D1221221

BY EDMUND T. DELANEY

NEW YORK'S TURTLE BAY OLD & NEW

Barre Publishers, Barre, Massachusetts

Library of Congress catalogue card number 65–16658
design: Shirley Errickson
composition: Commonwealth Press
printing: The Meriden Gravure Company

This book, I think, represents a new venture in books about New York—of which the number seems to increase unendingly—in that it deals with only a very limited area of the city. These few square blocks, however, have not only had a fascinating past, but hold a brilliant promise for the future.

I am indebted to many for advice and assistance. For support and encouragement I thank the noted New York architectural historian, Henry Hope Read, Jr.; the dynamic director of the Landmarks Preservation Commission, James Grote Van Derpool; Oliver Jensen, editor of American Heritage; *and Eugene Reynal; for editorial suggestions and improvements, Lowell K. Hanson, former president of the Turtle Bay Association; for technical and editorial advice, Barbara J. Snow, managing editor of* Antiques Magazine; *for comments and suggestions, the late Mabel Detmold of Turtle Bay Gardens, Emily Genauer of* The New York Herald Tribune *and William Lescaze F.A.I.A.; for a number of pictures in the book, my son, Nicholson Delaney, and for help in the selection of pictures, my daughter, Christopher.*

It is hoped that all credits have been duly acknowledged as they appear. However, particular thanks are due to Arthur B. Carlson and Betty J. Ezequelle, curator and assistant curator of prints at The New-York Historical Society; Albert K. Baragwanath, curator of prints at The Museum of the City of New York as well as other members of their staff, the office of Public Information of the United Nations, and the Durst Organization—particularly Irene F. Sussman.

Thanks are also expressed to Claire T. Hanrahan and Kathleen Maguire who typed (and retyped) the manuscript.

And then, as has often been written, "For their help, I am grateful, errors and omissions are mine alone."

Edmund T. Delaney

January 18, 1965. *New York City*

Cover: Section of New York City map published in 1776 from survey made by B. Ratzer, 1766–69. Turtle Bay appears at upper right.

Frontispiece: United Nations Headquarters (1960) from Welfare Island. In the background the Empire State Building to the immediate right of which is the United States Mission under construction.

Above: United States Mission to the U.N. at 799 United Nations Plaza.

CONTENTS.

FOREWORD.

As visitors and even residents look about the United Nations area in the 40's on the East Side, traditionally known as Turtle Bay, they would find it hard to believe that little more than 100 years ago this part of New York was largely farm land and that, in fact, it was the site of three of the finest farms in Old Manhattan with an original grant going back to the Dutch days.

Fifty years later, the character of the area had changed profoundly. In the early years of this century, Turtle Bay was mostly a deteriorating neighborhood of rundown brownstones interspersed among flour mills, tanneries, breweries and slaughterhouses. From north to south is was transversed by two elevated lines on Third and Second Avenues. Under the elevated structures, characterized by dust and rattling noises, was a conglomeration of bars, restaurants, second-hand stores and pawn shops on the street level with the upper floors mostly tenements.

New York, however, is always on the go. Now, another fifty years later, we find a residential neighborhood with restored brownstones interspersed among high, new apartment houses. The elevated tracks have disappeared and the saloons and taverns have now, in many cases, become elegant and expensive restaurants. Second-hand stores have generally been replaced with other purveyors of old goods which are now characterized as "antiques." Crosstown streets have been lined with trees. Supermarkets have taken the place of the old-time delicatessen shops. Fruit and meat vendors have disappeared. Along the East River is the great United Nations complex and the many new and elegant buildings devoted to various phases of public service. On Third Avenue and along East 42nd Street, the newest and many of the most glamorous commercial skyscrapers anywhere have made the eastern fringes of old Turtle Bay the business home of many of America's leading enterprises.

This, then, is the story of a small neighborhood of New York; one which extends from 41st Street to 51st Street and from the East River to Third Avenue. We shall call it Turtle Bay, even though some parts of these blocks may have fallen a few feet outside the wooden fences which marked Turtle Bay Farm at the end of the 18th Century.

The story of Turtle Bay is as old as that of New York itself. But it is much more than the story of just a neighborhood, for to a surprisingly large degree it reflects not only the history of the city but also that of the nation. Now and in the future it will more and more become a mirror to the entire globe, for it is in the halls of the United Nations in the old Turtle Bay Farm that the history of the world is now being unfolded day by day.

1

COLONIAL DAYS.

In colonial times, the Turtle Bay area, like the rest of the Island north of 14th Street, was an area of meadows and valleys with projecting rocks and hills which can still be seen only in Central Park. Around Turtle Bay itself (which was a cove from 45th to 48th Street, the present site of the United Nations Park) the area was swampy. Upper Manhattan was covered with farms and there were a good number of substantial mansions erected by city merchants who used them as summer places. There were clusters of small villages such as Stuyvesant Town, Yorkville, Bloomingdale, Manhattanville and Harlem. On the northwest corner of the Turtle Bay Farm was Odellville which was something of a rural community market area.

The Turtle Bay Farm, as it existed in the middle of the 18th Century, extended from 41st to 49th Street. It was bordered on the north by the Beekman Farm, on the east by the East River (with the cove from 45th to 48th Street), on the south by the Kips Bay Farm and on the west by the Eastern Post Road which came up from the old city, crossed into Third Avenue near 45th Street and then wound its way up to 50th Street between Third and Second Avenues. There it turned east to Second Avenue and then back toward Central Park, finally becoming the famous Boston Post Road. The irregular path of the old Eastern Post Road can be seen from the uneven line of the eastern side of the present Chrysler building and the unusual shape of the plot at 211 East 49th Street where a side of the inside court of Amster Yard still follows the old lines of the road. A series of milestones were erected in 1769 to mark distances along the road measured from Wall and Nassau Streets where City Hall was then located. These were reputedly placed under the personal supervision of Benjamin Franklin, who served as Deputy Postmaster General for the Colonies from 1753 to 1774. The fourth milestone was located on the north side of 46th Street just west of Third Avenue.

The southern part of Central Park was the source of a small creek, known as De Voor's Mill Stream, which ran into Turtle Bay at what is now the foot of the present 47th Street. The creek was crossed by the Eastern Post Road at 50th Street and Second Avenue at "Kissing Bridge No. 2," a well-known landmark of Old New York which existed until 1860. In 1759 an English clergyman, Andrew Burnaby[1], visited the colonies. The bridge is referred to in his journal with the comment that its name was derived from an accepted custom under which "it is part of the etiquette to salute the lady who has put herself under your protection." The first of these "Kissing Bridges" was at the intersection of Park Row and Pearl Street, while the third was at Third Avenue and 76th Street. De Voor's Mill Stream has been noted on maps of New York from the earliest days. One of these early maps is so remarkably accurate that it is still used in charting excavation for housing developments and skyscrapers. The president of one of these leading excavation companies in New York commented in 1964 on the old creek as follows:

Once Turtle Creek cut across the island from the southern edge of what's now Central Park to the foot of E. 46th St. The map showed it crossing Second Ave. at 48th St. We excavated for two apartment houses, on the northwest and southeast corners, and struck the creek underground exactly where the map showed it. The apartment built on the northeast corner missed it, as the map indicated it would.[2]

Whether or not "Turtle Bay" got its name because of the profusion of turtles in and around the cove seems to be open to question. The original name of the grant of the area south of the creek was "Deutal Bay Farm" and the first grant was made in 1639 by Dutch Governor William Kieft to two Englishmen, George Holmes and Thomas Hall, who were permitted to settle in New York after their capture by

1. *Kissing Bridge No. 2, showing creek running into Turtle Bay at 50th Street and Second Avenue on the Old Boston Road.*

S^R. PETER WARREN.

Vice Admiral Sir Peter Warren (1703–1752).

the Dutch in the repulse of an attacking force from Virginia in 1635. The original grant did not extend to the Post Road as did subsequent grants. "Deutal" was the Dutch word for a slightly bent blade (possibly inspired by the shape of the land), and there are those who claim that "Deutal" became anglicized into "Turtle." On the other hand, early settlers noted the profusion of the amphibians in the area and the good Doctor Burnaby himself tells that, in 1759, there were "several houses pleasantly situated upon East River, near New York, where it is common to have turtle feasts" and that these "happen once or twice in a week." Certainly by 1712 the name "Turtle Bay" had come into common usage as it is referred to in a will of that date and also in a deed in 1719.

Hall and Holmes originally undertook to develop a tobacco plantation on the property, but there is no evidence that this was ever done. In 1641 Hall sold out to his partner for "1,500 pounds of tobacco payable from the crop, which George shall make in 1641," but who can say whether the debt was ever discharged. It is known that by 1659 a saw mill had been established and small vessels were being built on the borders of the cove proper.

After New Amsterdam was taken over by the English in 1664, the Holmes property appeared to have been abandoned. In 1671, the then English Governor, Col. Francis Lovelace, having found that the land "doth not properly belong to any particular person," granted it over to a subordinate officer who apparently was one of his cronies, Capt. John Manning. The Governor's generosity to his friend also extended to Hogg Island, later knwon as Blackwell's Island and now Welfare Island.

Within two years, Manning had become second in command of the city. In 1673 in the course of the recurring wars between the Dutch and the British, the former almost inadvertently recaptured New York when the town was surrendered by Manning without firing a shot. It seems that the city had been stripped of its defenses, whether because of Manning's negligence or treachery we do not know. Valentine in his 1853 *History of the City of New York* recounts that after the British by virtue of a general peace treaty "again came into possession of the government, Manning was tried by court martial for cowardice and treachery; he was convicted, his sword broken over his head in front of the city-hall and himself incapacitated, from that time forward, from holding any station of trust or authority under his majesty."

Shortly thereafter, Holmes' heirs reasserted their title to the part of the land south of the creek and the title was confirmed. In 1676 the new Governor, Sir Edmund Andros, granted a substantial tract of land north of the creek to one Gabriel Carbosie. Different grants and deeds followed. Their status was often vague and varied. Some were recorded officially, some were merely delivered, while others simply overlapped previous grants. In any event, a large part of Turtle Bay was advertised for sale in the *New York Journal* of April 10, 1738, under the following description:

Also Forty four Acres of Land lying upon Manhatans Island, within four miles of this City, with a very good Grist Mill and two Bolting Mills, a large quantity of New Fencing stuff ready prepar'd for use, an old Orchard that maks Thirty Barrels of Syder, and Fifty young trees planted last Spring, all grafted for the best Kind of Fruits, being Part of Turtlebey, and formerly the place belonging to Theophilus Elseworth.

In the middle of the eighteenth century, Turtle Bay played an important role in the water commerce along the East River which was one of the principal lanes of traffic linking as it did New England and Long Island with Manhattan and New Jersey. The importance of the river as an artery of communication in colonial days can readily be appreciated in the light of the primitive conditions of the roads and the complete absence of bridges. Navigation in the East River was affected—then as now—by the ebb and flow of the tides and the unusually strong currents. The currents were especially swift along Blackwell's Island so that it was natural that many ships should avail themselves of the anchorage in adjoining Turtle Bay in order to await a favorable tide.

Apparently, a hulk had been used for the landing of cargoes at an early date for the records of the Common Council show that in 1734 one Captain Robert Long of H. M. S. *Seaford* applied to the Council for permission to remove the hulk and replace it with a new wharf. This request was granted and it was agreed that the Captain should:

erect thereon at his own expense a wharf convenient for his Majesties ships to careen at and remove the hulk aforesaid and such other wrecks as lie within said Turtle Bay, the object being to make the Bay more useful and commodious for the sheltering of a far greater number of shipping therein, and more especially to secure them in Winter from the driving ice of the River.

James Beekman (1732–1807).

In 1749, the larger part of the Farm south of the creek was acquired by Sir Peter Warren, who was a prominent British Naval officer then holding the rank of Vice Admiral. Warren had distinguished himself in the battles of Louisberg in 1745 and Cape Finisterre in 1747 for which he received the Cross of Bath. He had married into the De Lancey family, settled in New York where he had extensive holdings and resided in Greenwich Village. He had apparently hoped to become Governor of the Province, but he died in 1752. A monument was erected to him in Westminster Abbey with an epitaph written by Dr. Samuel Johnson: *Knight of the Bath, Vice Admiral of the Red Squadron of the British Fleet and Member of Parliament for the City and Liberty of Westminster.*

Fourteen years later the northern part of the Turtle Bay Farm was acquired by James Beekman along with some land included in the Carbosie grant. These parcels became known as the Beekman Farm which extended what is now 49th Street to 51st Street and the Post Road to the River. James Beekman (1732–1807) then built his famous mansion *Mount Pleasant* near 51st Street and First Avenue. For over a hundred years *Mount Pleasant* stood as one of the great and historic mansions of New York. In 1840, with the opening of First Avenue, the house was moved to 50th Street to make way for the opening of 51st Street. It was finally torn down in 1874. Fortunately, a parlor and a bedroom from the house along with three original mantels have been preserved and can still be seen at The New-York Historical Society.

The Turtle Bay Farm was retained by the heirs of Sir Peter Warren up through the Revolution. At that time the property contained four or five houses, a shipyard, and a wharf at the foot of 45th Street on which there was a stone house used as a military storehouse. This latter structure had been the scene of a "hit and run" raid in 1775 by the so-called "Liberty Boys" who took a sloop from Greenwich, Connecticut, through the turbulent waters of Hell Gate, seized the house from the British guards and took some military stores back to Boston for use by the Continental Army. The leaders of the raiding party were Marinus Willet, who was later to become mayor of New York, and Isaac Sears, a friend of James Beekman, who later became a prominent New York merchant.

To the south of Turtle Bay Farm was the Kips Bay Farm which originated in a grant from the Dutch Governor to Jacobus Kip, secretary of the Council of New Amsterdam. In 1655, Kip erected an important house at 35th Street and Second Avenue with bricks believed to have been imported from Holland. The Kip family continued to live in this house for nearly 200 years. When demolished in 1851, it was the last of the old "boweries" of the Dutch era and was considered at the time to be the oldest house in Manhattan.

By the end of the Colonial era, what is now Midtown Manhattan bordering on the East River must surely have been a pleasant spot with a series of farms and graceful homes having easy access by the Post Road to the city proper. Cato's Tavern on the Post Road near 54th Street and Second Avenue was already well established and known for the dinner and supper parties held there. Reverting back to our friendly visitor from England, Doctor Burnaby, we learn that life in these parts was not unpleasant in 1759:

Thirty or forty gentlemen and ladies meet and dine together; drink tea in the afternoon; fish and amuse themselves till evening, and then return home in Italian chaises (the fashionable carriage in this and most parts of America . . .), a gentleman and a lady in each chaise.

Burnaby also noted that in New York the "women are handsome and agreeable, though rather more reserved than the Philadelphia ladies."

1. *"Mount Pleasant" built by James Beekman in 1763–64 and demolished in 1874.* **Beekman** *family coach shown opposite.*

2. *"Old Store House." Scene of the 1775 raid by the Liberty Boys.*

1/2

1

2

THE REVOLUTION.

THE BUCOLIC TRANQUILITY of Turtle Bay was shattered by the impact of the Revolutionary War. After the American Army had been disastrously defeated on Long Island, it was weary and disheartened. Washington then withdrew from Long Island and fell back to Manhattan, crossing the East River in the fog on August 29, 1776, and landing in the present United Nations area. The Americans had built fortifications along the East River, although one British officer reported that they were more calculated to "amuse" than to defend. It seems that the New England contingent of Washington's Army wanted to burn New York City and then withdraw to New England. The local New Yorkers and the New Jerseyites were not so ready to destroy the city even though it was known to be a hotbed of Tories. Washington sought instructions from the Congress, and he was told to preserve the city in the eventuality that the Americans would take it over again. Bronze bells and bell clappers were removed from belfries and dispatched to Newark so that they would not fall into British hands, but despite all this, a fire, set by accident or by design, actually did destroy a large part of the city.

The Americans did not have long to tarry on Manhattan Island. They were followed closely by substantial British forces which, under cover of the guns of five men of war, landed in front of the Kip house in Kips Bay on September 15, 1776. Little resistance was encountered. In Washington's own words, many of his men "ran without firing a shot."

Sir William Howe, the British Commander-in-Chief, did not pursue his opponents with any great vigor, but preferred to linger and accept the hospitality of the famous Mrs. Murray who gave a party at Inclenberg, the farm of the wealthy Quaker merchant, Robert Murray, located at approximately Park Avenue and 37th Street. The story of Mrs. Murray's hospitality has been the subject of many novels and plays. Whether or not the tea party was planned with ulterior motives, the fact remains that while Sir William, Sir Henry Clinton and Lord Cornwallis and their subordinate officers were enjoying this hospitality, a substantial part of Washington's army under General Israel Putnam escaped to the northern end of Manhattan with the guidance of Aaron Burr, who apparently even then was fairly adept at finding devious paths to ultimate safety.

One of the Hessian officers has described the landing as follows:

We landed about four miles from New York City. . . . I was most of the time near the East River, along whose banks are the most beautiful homes. I had the honor of taking possession of these handsome dwellings and also of the enemy's battery, where I found five cannon. The rebels fled in every direction. All of these houses were filled with furniture and other valuable articles, lawful prices of war; but the owners had fled leaving all their slaves behind. In a day or two after, however, one head of the family after another appeared, and tears of joy and thankfulness rolled down the cheeks of these happy people, when to their great surprise, they found their houses, fruits, animals and furniture intact and learned from me that I had only taken possession of them for their protection.

Not all of the houses, however, were returned to the owners. As the Beekman House was one of the most prominent homes in the area and owned, moreover, by a prominent patriot, James Beekman, the British took it over. It was occupied successively by Sir William Howe, Sir Henry Clinton and Sir Guy Carleton as their headquarters until they finally withdrew from Manhattan in 1783 after the Treaty of Paris. The Beekman greenhouse was the scene of the trial and sentencing, on September 21, 1776, of Nathan Hale who had been captured the previous day in the vicinity of the Dove Tavern on the west

1. *General Sir Henry Clinton (1738–1795). His signature appears at the left.*
2. *Nathan Hale at Beekman House after his capture.*

side of Third Avenue at 66th Street. Hale at one time was believed to have been executed on what is today the site of the United Nations, but it is now recognized that he gave his life for the cause near Dove Tavern where he had been captured.

It was also at Beekman House in 1780 that Major John André received his final instructions before he departed on his attempt to meet with Benedict Arnold in the betrayal of West Point.

In 1780, Beekman House was occupied by Baroness Frederika von Riedesel, the attractive wife of the General in command of the Hessian troops who had been captured at Saratoga. The Baroness was a leading light in the Loyalist society circles in New York and equally admired by distinguished American patriots for her charm and graciousness as well as her beauty. The Baroness was invited to occupy the house by Sir Henry Clinton and she moved in the midst of what was probably a real winter blizzard. She has given a vivid account of it in her "Journals" reporting snow drifts of eight feet and mentioning balustrades collapsing under the weight of the snow.

Major John André (1751–1780). A self-portrait made in his cell the morning of his execution.

The Baroness wrote of this time and of the succeeding summer: *. . . the small-pox was raging violently in the city. . . .*

. . . At the end of the winter General Tryon sailed for England, but just before his departure, he sent to my house, unbeknown to me, magnificent furniture, tapestry, carpets, and curtains, besides a set of silk hangings for an entire room. . . .

About this time our friendly relations began with our excellent friend General Clinton, who was the general-in-chief of the English army in the southern provinces of America. . . . His country residence was magnificent, a most beautiful situation orchard and meadow, and the . . . river running directly in front of the house. Everything was placed at our disposal, including fruits of the most delicious flavor; indeed, of this latter article we had more than we could eat. Our servants feasted on peaches even to satiety, and our horses, which roamed through the orchards, eagerly ate the fruit from the trees, disdaining that upon the ground, which every evening we had gathered up and given to the pigs to fatten them. It seems almost incredible, but nevertheless it is true, that with nothing but this fruit we fattened six pigs, the flesh of which was capital, only the fat was somewhat soft. Peach, apricot, and other fruit-trees, are raised here, without espaliers, and have trunks as thick as those of ordinary trees.

Not far from us were the Hell-gates, which are dangerous breakers for those ships that pass through them up the river. We often saw ships in danger, but only one was wrecked and went to pieces during our stay at this place.

General Clinton came often to visit us, but in hunter's dress, accompanied by only one aid-de-camp. . . . The last time he came to see us, he had with him the unfortunate—as he afterwards became—Major André, who, the day afterward, set out upon the fatal expedition, in which he was captured by the Americans, and afterwards hung as a spy. It was very sad that this preeminently excellent young man should have fallen a victim to his zeal and his kind heart, which led him to undertake such a precarious errand instead of leaving it to older and known officers, to whom properly the duty belonged, but on whom on that very account (as they would be more exposed to danger), he wished to save.

We passed much of our time at this most agreeable place; but our contentment was broken in upon by a malignant fever [*probably a virulent form of malaria*], *that prevailed in New-York and of which, in our family alone, twenty fell ill; eight dangerously. Among these eight were my husband and my daughter Gustava. . . . every day persons would tell me of fifty or sixty fresh burials, which certainly did not tend to raise my spirits. The heat which the sick suffered was so intense that their pulse beat one hundred and thirty-five times in a minute. All our servants were sick, . . . At night I was often busied in making for my patients a lemonade of salts of wormwood mixed with lemon juice, sugar and water. By which means, as all the sick in the house had them, I used up in the space of two weeks, two full boxes of lemons, each box containing five hundred.*

. . . The pastor, Mylius, and our trusty yager, Rockel, both of whom remained well, assisted me by turns watching at night. . . . At length all of our household who were sick were restored to health, and not one died, a result that abundantly paid me for all my trouble.

We remained the entire summer of 1780, upon this lovely estate.—Baroness Riedesel, *Letters and Journals* (trans. by Stone, 1867), 1777–87.

After peace was proclaimed in 1783, James Beekman returned to *Mount Pleasant,* but then in good Yankee fashion proceeded to rent it to the British commander in chief, Sir Guy Carleton, who spent six months working out the evacuation of New York. This was an enormous undertaking for in addition to the British Troops, it has been estimated that there were 10,000 native New Yorker Loyalists and some 30,000 other Loyalists to evacuate, almost all of whom eventually went to Nova Scotia. Finally on November 25, 1783, the last British ship left and the Americans entered the city in a formal procession. The American officers and staff, presumably including Washington, were entertained at *Mount Pleasant* "in the drawing room with punch made with lemons plucked from trees growing in the green-house" and Washington, thereafter, was a frequent visitor while in New York.

After the Revolution, James Beekman made some substantial changes in the mansion, building an octagonal room with a handsomely carved mantel and furnishing a parlor with oil paintings, fine chairs and sofas covered in Beauvais Tapestry. Some of these furnishings are still to be seen at the New-York Historical Society.

Meanwhile, after the death of Sir Peter Warren, the Turtle Bay estate was divided among his two daughters and his granddaughter. The latter obtained this part of Turtle Bay as a result of the drawing of lots between interested heirs. She sold her interest in 1791 to Francis Bayard Winthrop, a prominent New York merchant who at the same time acquired a small parcel north of the creek. Winthrop built a large frame house known as *Prospect Mansion* at First Avenue and 41st Street. This house existed only until the 1850's when First Avenue was cut through the knoll on which it stood. The term "Prospect Place," presently used in the Tudor City enclave, is derived from Winthrop's mansion.

Baroness Frederika Von Riedesel (1746–1808).

Turtle Bay and Blackwell's Island about 1840 at the foot of what now is 49th Street. In the background is the Beekman House and to the right the rocks where Poe went for his "afternoon swim."

RURAL NEW YORK.

EARLY IN 1807 street plans were laid out covering most of Manhattan Island in symmetrical gridiron fashion. The earliest known map of New York showing the present streets was made in 1811 at the instruction of Mayor DeWitt Clinton. Great discussions were held on the merits of the plan. It was attacked as providing for a city with a population greater than any "this side of China," but the commissioners defended the plan stating that it was very possible that within the next 100 years all of Manhattan would be fairly settled. In this they proved to be correct, but they were less foresighted when they failed to provide for sufficient parks and open spaces. Criticisms were leveled at them at the time, but they defended their cause on the grounds of economy stating that Manhattan was so well surrounded by water and good recreational lands that it was unnecessary to make provision on the Island itself. It was this plan that accounted for the monotonous layout of Manhattan Island and it was bitterly opposed by many property owners. The effects of the plan 100 years later were well described by I. N. Phelps Stokes in his classic work on Manhattan, *The Iconography of Manhattan Island,* Volume 4, page 407, as follows:

Unfortunately, this plan, although possessing the merits of simplicity and directness, lacked entirely the equally essential elements of variety and picturesqueness, which demand a large degree of respect for the natural conformation of the land. The new plan was entirely deficient in sentiment and charm, and with its gradual development, little by little, the individuality, the interest, and the beauty of one choice spot after another have been swept away until, now, except in Central Park and at the extreme north of the Island, scarcely anything remains to remind us of the primitive beauty and the fascinating diversity of natural charms which we know Manhattan once possessed.

In the first part of the 19th Century, "progress" was gradual. Upper New York was divided into lots about 1830. The area north of 34th Street, however, remained predominantly rural, although the large farms and estates were gradually being broken up and sold in plots and parcels of varying sizes. The more fortunate overlooked the East River which was full of thriving activity as the principal route of communication between New York and New England. There was a bustling traffic of sailboats and horse wheel ferries soon to be supplanted by steam power. It was in the East River at the southern extremity of the Old Turtle Bay Farm that Robert Fulton in 1808 had held his first trials to prove that boats driven by steam were a distinct possibility. The bucolic river scene remained uninterrupted during the War of 1812 because plans to fortify the area to prevent the reoccurrence of any British landings came to naught. No fortification was instituted nor was a shot ever fired.

It was to rural Turtle Bay that both Horace Greeley and Edgar Allen Poe repaired for quiet country living. In 1841 Greeley had started the famed *New York Daily Tribune.* At this time he was suffering grave family tragedies. Mrs. Greeley had lost several children and was in poor health and in a nervous and upset condition. A new son had just been born and Greeley bought seven acres along Turtle Bay itself between East 48th and 49th Streets. He had great difficulty retaining household help because servants found it difficult to endure Mrs. Greeley's treatment of them. Greeley complained that he had to do all the work around the house and, in fact, he called it "Castle Doleful." His biographers tell us that he was frequently away on trips. The farm was described by Margaret Fuller,[3] his friend and associate on the *Tribune* who was also a good friend of Emerson, Hawthorne and Poe:

The place is, to me, entirely country, and all around is so bold and free. It is two miles or more from the thickly settled parts of New York. Stopping on the Harlem Road, you enter a lane nearly a quarter of a mile long, and going by a small brook and pond that locks in the place, and ascending a slightly rising ground, get sight of the house, which, old fashioned and of mellow tint, fronts on a flower garden filled with shrubs, large vines and trim box borders. Passing through a wide hall you come out on a piazza stretching the whole length of the house, where one can walk in all weathers; and thence by a step or two, on a lawn with picturesque masses of rocks, shrubs and trees overlooking the East River. . . . The beauty here seen by moonlight is truly transporting.[4]

Turtle Bay did not relieve Greeley's sorrows. First his daughter died, and the death of his newly born son followed in 1850. Stricken by the new tragedy, Greeley moved back to Greenwich Village.

Margaret Fuller herself, a few years before her marriage and subsequent tragic death in a shipwreck, spent much time at Turtle Bay. After completing *Woman of the Nineteenth Century,* she worked for Greeley on the Tribune and lived with the family. At that time Blackwell's Island was a prison and, an ardent reformer, Margaret Fuller made it her business to visit it, which she did by rowboat from Turtle Bay accompanied by William Channing.[5]

In the spring of 1846, Edgar Allen Poe, who had borrowed money from Greeley, amongst others, and who was on the verge of a complete breakdown, took a house near 47th Street facing Turtle Bay with his wife, Virginia, who was desperately ill. The Poe house was not far from the John Miller farmhouse. Sarah, daughter of Miller, some years later wrote:

When I was a little girl we lived in a house facing Turtle Bay, on the East River, near the present 47th Street. Among our nearest neighbors was a charming family . . . consisting of Mr. Poe, his wife, Virginia, and his mother-in-law, Mrs. Clemm. Because Virginia was very ill, at this time, I never saw her leave home. Poe and Mrs. Clemm would frequently call on us. He would also run over every little while to ask my father to lend him our row-boat, and then he would enjoy himself pulling at the oars over to the little islands just south of Blackwell's Island for his afternoon swim.[6]

Poe stayed only a few months in Turtle Bay. His wife's condition increasingly deteriorated and it was found advisable to return to Fordham. However, he retained the friendship of the Millers who visited the family there on several occasions. Virginia died in 1847 and Poe himself completely collapsed in Baltimore in 1849.

The Miller farmhouse itself was described later by Sarah Miller's brother as follows:

Our home, when we became acquainted with Mr. Poe and his wife and mother, was at the foot of 47th Street, East River, New York. It was an attractive place at that time, no house within a quarter of a mile of it. We had five acres of ground beautifully laid out with shade and fruit trees in great variety

Edgar Allen Poe (1809–1849).

1. *Cato's Tavern on the Old Boston Post Road. Erected 1712, demolished 1853.*
2. *Turtle Bay in 1853.*

Horace Greeley (1811–1872), editor, journalist and statesman; founder of the "Daily Tribune" and unsuccessful candidate for president against Gen. U. S. Grant in 1872.

on the river front known as "Turtle Bay" affording a fine opportunity for boating, fishing, bathing and swimming. All of these Poe enjoyed exceedingly. I may add he was a great swimmer and I well remember some of his antics in the water. In the spring of 1846, Mr. Poe came to our house in search of a desirable place for his invalid wife and was so taken with the commodious house; large airy rooms, flowering vines over the porches, fresh fruit, eggs, milk and butter, and river privileges, in the use of our boat that he prevailed on my parents to accommodate them until he could find a place where they could keep house for themselves.[7]

Although we have no precise record of Nathaniel Hawthorne having visited his friends Greeley, Poe or Margaret Fuller, who were living in the area at the time, or James W. Beekman (1815–1877), who in 1837 had inherited *Mount Pleasant,* he undoubtedly knew the house for he noted in his *American Notebook* the moving of the Beekman House in 1850 from 51st to 50th Street because of the opening of First Avenue:

A sketch—the devouring of the old country residence by the overgrown monster of the City. For instance, Mr. Beekman's ancestral residence was originally several miles from the city of New York; but the pavements kept creeping nearer and nearer; till now the house is removed, and a street runs directly through what was once its hall.

The expansion of the city to the north resulted in the gradual paving of the large avenues. Horsecar lines were established. Third Avenue, during the second quarter of the 19th Century became known colloquially as Macadamized Road and was described by Dayton in his *Last Days of Knickerbocker Life in New York* as "the trotting road over which our sires exercised their favorite nags." However a bend in the Old Post Road from 45th to 65th Street was for some time kept open and became known as Cato's Lane.

Dayton also describes Cato's Tavern, still thriving in the 1840's but demolished in 1853:

The quaint old barroom and diminutive sitting room with their sanded floors were scrupulously neat; the coarse, whitewashed walls covered with odd engravings of the olden time, would prove rare curiosities today. But they, with their proprietor, have long since passed away. Piles of brick and mortar now occupy the site where Cato daily dispensed creature comforts to the Hones, Carters, Beekmans, Tallmadges, Janeways, Van Cortlandts and others with their many friends.

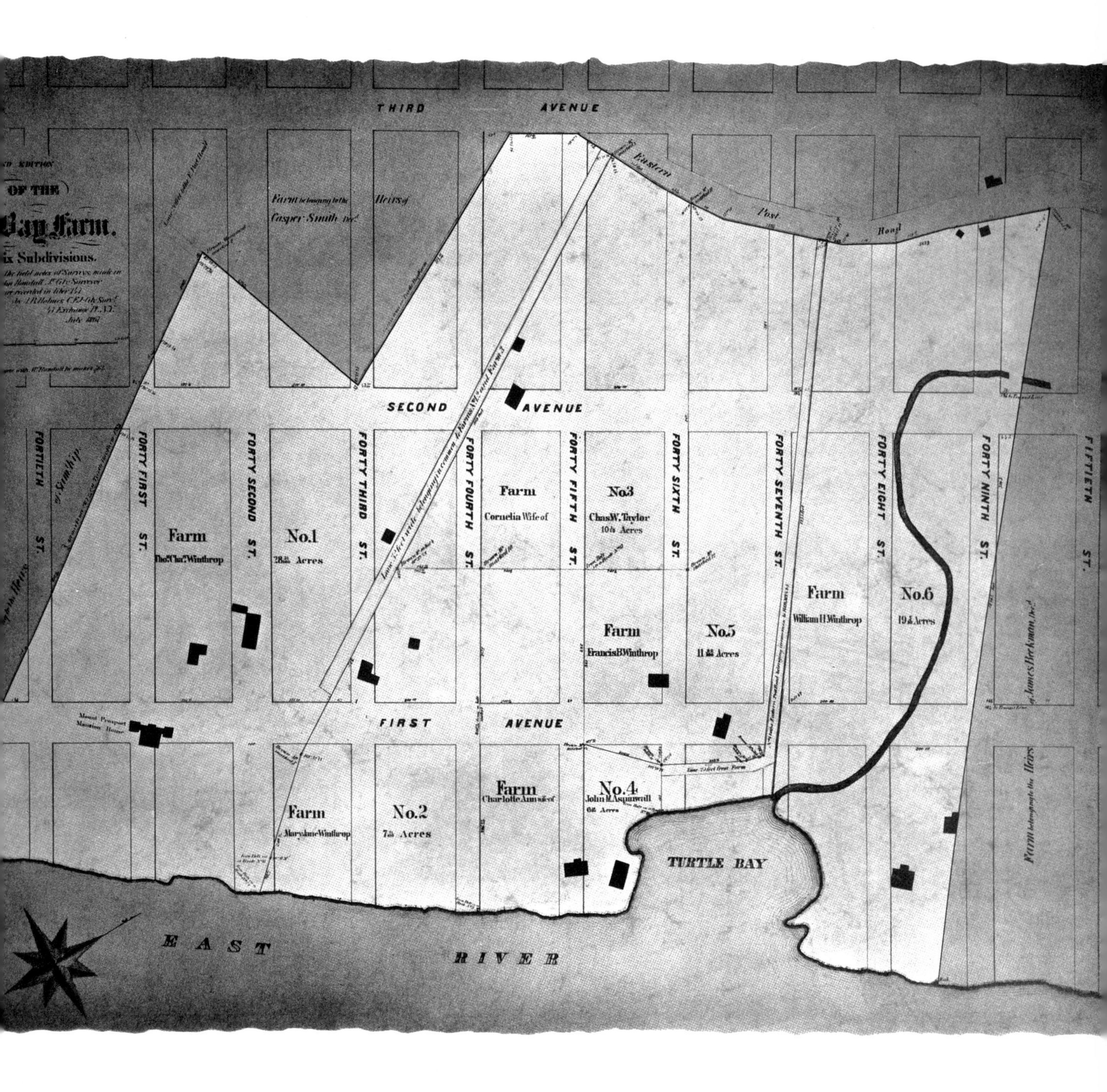

Turtle Bay and its six subdivisions. From a map made in 1820.

Building brownstones in 1868 on East 46th Street looking west from Third Avenue.

THE BROWNSTONE ERA.

FROM 1840 TO 1850 large avenues continued to be opened up to the north and cross streets were graded. James W. Beekman, who was to have a distinguished career as a New York Senator and public servant and philanthropist, soon realized that the days of the mansions and the farms were numbered and he embarked on a broad plan to develop his property through the sale of small plots for private residences. Water mains and sewers were installed and parts of the streets were graded. A school district was established. Beekman made financing arrangements available to prospective builders and buyers. On 50th Street he acquired various plots to round out his holdings. By 1862, Beekman's properties were valued at $343,000 which, in terms of the then value of the dollar, represented an enormous investment. It was as such that Beekman regarded his holdings because, in 1857, he himself had moved out of the mansion to live at 5 East 34th Street where he bought a town house. This acquisition was to be followed in 1863 by the purchase of a summer home in Oyster Bay.

Mindful of the need for a well-rounded residential area, Beekman, an ardent Dutch Reformed Churchman, in 1859 gave land as well as financial assistance for a church on 50th Street. The deed, however, contained a covenant that if ever the property should not be used as a church, it was to revert to the Beekman heirs. In consequence there is now a successor church, the Reformed Episcopal Church on 50th Street, which was built into a substantial apartment house thus deriving income from the property and yet preserving the title.

The Turtle Bay area south of the Beekman property was developed on a more haphazard basis and it was not restricted to residential use. Old maps show match factories, carriage houses, carpentry shops, mills and a good number of breweries. Even before the Civil War on 42nd Street, east of Third Avenue in the general area of the Daily News Building and Tudor City, there was a large settlement of squatters who lived in broken-down shanties known as Goat Hill because of the goats kept by the shanty dwellers. The hill was also known as "Paddy Corcoran's Roost" after a notorious thug who dominated the squatters, a good number of whom had spent some time in the City Penitentiary then located on Blackwell's Island. The banks of Turtle Bay itself became something of a dumping place and shanty town. By 1868 the bay was filled in.

During the Civil War, New Yorkers were less than unanimous in their support and enthusiasm for the Union cause. In March, 1863, the first Draft Act was passed and an enrollment office was established at Third Avenue and 46th Street. The office was opened on July 11, 1863, and enrollments were peaceful on the first day. On the following Monday, however, a mob assembled south of Central Park and marched down to 46th Street where a riot began that lasted over three days. Within two hours, the entire block between 45th and 46th Street was destroyed. The riots spread to other areas and it was necessary to call upon the troops to disperse the mobs. These draft riots in New York were among the most severe ever to take place within the United States. Among the looters were the residents of "Paddy Corcoran's Roost" who were quick to take advantage of such a fortuitous opportunity. The riots lasted four days during which eighteen Negroes were lynched, the Colored Orphan Asylum on Fifth Avenue was burned, twelve hundred persons were killed and over eight thousand were injured.

It was after the Civil War that building activity commenced in earnest. Brownstones were built block by block, all of a uniform pattern. The entrance was marked by a stoop about eight feet above the sidewalk level leading into a hall from which one entered the formal living room, and then the family parlor in the rear. The ceilings were high and the windows were long and narrow. The front room in the basement was the family dining room and the rear room was the kitchen which opened out into a yard used for the drying of laundry and the storage of wood and coal. On the floor above the parlor

1. *Second Avenue looking north from 42nd Street toward Beekman Hill in 1*

2. *Civil War Draft riots in 1863 on First Av*

floor were two master bedrooms with a little hall bedroom over the stairs usually used by the youngest child. The top floor had small bedrooms for other children and two bedrooms for domestic help—which in those days was readily available in exchange for food, shelter and nominal wages. The only plumbing facilities were on the second floor. The hall stairway was rounded and there was a niche between the first and second floors popularly called "coffin corner," allegedly so placed as to permit a full-size casket to be carried up into the front parlor which was reserved for christenings, betrothals, formal receptions and wakes.

In 1865, the natural drainage afforded by De Voor's Mill Stream was obstructed by embankments and new streets. The waters backed up and the old stream area became notoriously unhealthy giving rise to an incidence of typhoid. In 1854, Mrs. Beekman had contracted cholera and the doctors warned Beekman against his wife's living at *Mount Pleasant* so close to the East River. This was undoubtedly one more reason for his departure in 1857. Underground drainage was finally built in 1871 and a subterranean stream made to pass, as it still does, through a sewer nine feet in diameter into the East River at 49th Street.

Hon. James W. Beekman (1815–1877).

3. *Dumping ground at foot of East 47th Street about 1865. Then described as one of the "pest spots of the Metropolis," this is the present site of the United Nations.*

WAITING FOR THE FIVE CENT TRAIN.

A THEATRE PARTY

DECLINE AND FALL.

THE 1870's SAW horsecars in full use on Second and Third Avenues. The Beekman mansion was demolished in 1874. Fourth Avenue, now Park Avenue, was covered with railroad tracks leading into Grand Central. In a more elegant section of town, beyond the tracks, St. Patrick's Cathedral was in the course of erection and Columbia College was established on 49th Street near Madison Avenue.
Along the East River, however, deterioration had set in. Brownstones at the eastern end of 43rd Street had backyards sloping gradually toward the river with its enormous traffic including regular commutation boats carrying commuters from their downtown place of business to their country homes in the 80's and 90's and further up into Harlem. As First Avenue developed, these backyards disappeared. Between 1880 and 1900 the east side of First Avenue, an area which once had been one of the delightful coves of Manhattan Island, became the site of abattoirs and meat packaging houses. These supplied the entire island of Manhattan until after the Second World War when the slaughterhouses were torn down to make way for the United Nations.
The closer to the river the greater the deterioration. The southern part of the Beekman property which remained in family hands (James W. Beekman died in 1877) was leased to a coal dealer. The East 40's eventually became dead-end streets lined with factories, garages, coal pockets and power houses, ending with cattle pens, abattoirs and packing houses, dilapidated wharves and railroad freight piers where the cattle were unloaded.
Third and Second Avenues formed vital north-south arteries on the East Side. However, horsecars and horsecarts ended up in hopeless traffic congestions. Many plans were proposed to solve the vital traffic problem, one of which was a "moving sidewalk" in the form of an endless belt laid over the sidewalk. After much discussion, the city finally adopted a street railway system which was to have steam engines and passenger cars running on an elevated steel trestle built over the avenue. The proposal met with violent opposition not only on the part of property owners who clearly foresaw the fall in values of property situated on the avenues, but also from various groups who made dire prophecies of fires which would be caused by ashes on the street and trains falling off the tracks. There were those who conjectured that the "El" would constitute "a continuous long ride for Peeping Toms." In spite of the opposition, the El became a reality and in 1878, amidst great acclaim and celebration, the first train left Hanover Square in lower Manhattan and proceeding along Third Avenue arrived at Grand Central fifteen minutes later on August 15, 1878. To quote a contemporary account in Frank Leslie's *Illustrated Weekly:*

The line of the New York Elevated Railroad on the east-side of the city having been completed, excursion trains passed over it on August 15th, starting at Hanover Square, in front of the Cotton Exchange, and going directly to the Grand Central Depot Elevated Station. The distance from Hanover Square to Forty-second Street was made in fifteen minutes.
Through Pearl Street and Franklin Square the pioneer train was run at a moderate rate of speed,

1. *Character sketches on the Elevated Railway.*

1
2 | 3

passing between the piers which are a part of the support of the approach to the Brooklyn Bridge. Beyond this point in the New Bowery the road passes over low ground, and, to make an even grade, is built at an unusual height above the pavement. Along the Bowery and Third Avenue the windows of the houses were filled with faces, and pedestrians paused to watch the train as it rattled by. Turning into Forty-second Street, the excursionists were introduced to luncheon laid out in the Station which directly adjoins the Grand Central Depot, Grand Union Hotel, and other prominent uptown buildings. The time on the return trip was thirteen minutes to Fulton Street.

In 1880, the Second Avenue line was completed to 67th Street, and soon thereafter both lines were completed to the Harlem River.

The El stations and cars were thus described in the *Illustrated Weekly*—a description which later-day patrons of the El would find it difficult to visualize from their memories of the dilapidated El stations and broken-down cars:

The interior of both the ladies' and gentlemen's waiting rooms are to be very tastefully furnished and finished throughout in what is known as the Eastlake style of decoration. . . . The exterior of each station is to be ornamented with iron pilasters and decorated panels of the same metal. . . . The general style of the exterior of the buildings with their many gables, ventilators, finials, etc. might be properly classed as modification of the Renaissance and Gothic styles of architecture, presenting somewhat the appearance of a Swiss villa. The glass ventilators are to be in variegated colors and ornamental bay windows in the waiting rooms are to afford a view of the street below. . . . Cars are being constructed at the Pullman Palace Car Works at Detroit, Mich. Each car has seating capacity for 64 people. The woodwork of the doors, seats and sides of the cars is of mahogany and the ceiling is paneled with oak and mahogany. The seats are furnished with flexible backs of maroon morocco, and spring bottoms with cushions of morocco for Winter use, and in Summer to be covered with woven rattan. The floors are to be covered with heavy Axminster rug and carpets.

Although the elevated railroads performed a vital function in the communication system of the city, they did not improve the streets on which they were built. Light and sunshine were shut out and replaced by soot and noise, dirt and dinginess. Third Avenue and, to a lesser extent, Second Avenue became street slums with cold water flats, pawn shops, bars and grills with occasional delicatessens, vegetable and meat shops.

Beekman Hill remained a secluded residential neighborhood, but to the south slums were developing. By the end of the 19th Century, the brownstones, while never sumptuous or elegant but still comfortable homes, had begun to deteriorate and many of the families who had built them moved into other more elegant neighborhoods.

Thus it was in the early years of this century that many of the brownstones in the upper 40's were turned into rooming houses. They were decorated with fire escapes which, in turn, were graced by laundry and small items of food kept on the escape in the absence of ice boxes. Some of the brownstones had given way to the so-called "railroad flats"—walk-up tenements of some 6 or 7 flights with small connecting rooms. Here were crowded large families usually four to a floor. The first floors of these buildings were turned into store fronts or neighborhood restaurants.

The neighborhood was populated by many ethnic groups so well portrayed by Sholem Asch[8] in his *East River,* published in 1946, and so accurately descriptive of the early 20th Century in the area. The old families of Colonial lineage had long departed, the middle class was in the process of moving away and most of the residents were newly arrived immigrants seeking a better life in the new world.

1. *Third Avenue elevated trains with steam engines about 1880 showing remodeled Car Barn with new Victorian façade. Now the site of Manhattan House.*

2. *Third Avenue horsecars at same Car Barn in 1873 before remodeling.*

3. *Interior of a passenger car on the Elevated Railway.*

One brownstone at 238 East 48th Street was the first building used by The Travelers Aid Society from 1907 to 1914. It was to this building, that lost travelers were brought from Grand Central and other stations and ferry boat piers.

East of Second Avenue between 41st and 47th Streets the population was predominantly Italian. German and Irish prevailed on the west side of Second Avenue. Forty-eighth and 49th Streets east of Second Avenue were largely Jewish. Between Second and Third Avenues there were various groups somewhat more prosperous than their neighbors to the east. This was true especially of 50th and 51st Streets and even more so of Beekman Place where the property restrictions laid down by Beekman had preserved the residential character of the neighborhood.

The compactness of ethnic groups is illustrated by two separate Catholic churches within one hundred yards of each other near 47th Street and Second Avenue—one for the Germans and one for the Italians. Other groups also had separate places of worship as well as separate pubs and taverns largely patronized by their members.

Speaking of a block of 48th Street near the River in the early days of the century and about a cast of characters which included Irish, Jews, Italians, Germans, Poles and Hungarians, Asch describes the area as follows:

The street was a city in itself, in a world of its own. The people who lived in it knew each other and were interested in each other. All of them took part in the block's affairs. . . .

* * *

The inhabitants of 48th Street fell into two categories. There were those who came and went, occupying for a short period the usually empty flats in one of the buildings of the long uniform row of three-story houses that lined part of both sides of the street. These were mostly down-at-the-heel theater folk, small-bit actors, musicians, and stage hands, who worked in the theatrical section farther west in Manhattan and whom poverty had driven to the cheaper neighborhood of the East River. Their places of residence changed with their 'engagements.' They weren't looked on as properly part of the local population. . . .

* * *

To the same category belonged the residents who were waiters in the elegant restaurants in the swanky sections of the city, and all of those who had jobs around the city's night life, over toward Broadway. The other category was represented by the 'old settlers,' the permanent residents, the backbone of the block, who knew one another, loved or hated one another, but belonged together.

* * *

The streets ended in 'dead ends' hemmed in by fences erected by the owners of the feed storehouses and stables. In a couple of places, however, there was an old unused dock, the planks water soaked and rotted. From these docks one could hear the splashing of children swimming close to the shore, driven to find relief from the overpowering heat, disregarding the perils of the holes and falling timbers of the dock.[9]

The people in the neighborhood or at least the "old settlers" all went off to work early in the morning and returned late at night for in those days there was no 7- or 8-hour day or 5-day week. Indeed, a number of the young girls in Asch's novel worked in the garment industry and were caught in the famous Triangle Fire of 1908 which jolted the civic conscience of New York and resulted in great reforms in labor conditions. The manner in which all these people went to and from their work is well-described in the story:

. . . All the trolleys on First Avenue were packed with human freight, the passengers pushed together, one holding onto the other to avoid falling off the car which raced along in the morning rush hour with a special confusion, noise, and clanging.

There seemed to be no end to the hordes pouring out toward First Avenue, no beginning or end to the long line of trolley cars, all crowded to the running boards. The street leading to the Second Avenue El station was thick with people. But they were there only for a while; soon they had dis-

Travelers Aid Society (1909) at 238 East 48th Street.

appeared as though the pavement had opened up and swallowed them. New throngs appeared, a riot of black-red-white-gray dots, to be swallowed in their turn by the open steps of the El station. Above, on the tracks, one El train after another raced along like an iron monster, splitting the ears with the deafening clatter of iron wheels on iron rails. Trains stopped at the station with a grinding and creaking of brakes, the passengers squeezed together in a tight mass. The structure covered the avenue like an iron roof, shutting out the light of day.

At the end of 49th Street was a pier which is still to be seen and which served as a favorite bathing spot. Beekman Hill was rocky, but a few blocks to the north was the BAB beach so called because of the bare exposure of the lower rear anatomy of all the male patrons. All of the river bank is now covered by the Franklin D. Roosevelt Drive.

While the upper 40's and lower 50's still continued to be residential, the lower 40's became increasingly commercial. Many taverns and restaurants became newspaper hangouts. Other trades of the area were paint, hardware and small machinery. By the end of World War I, there was little to recommend the area. By then it had become one of the least attractive sections of a rapidly growing metropolis. Its only asset was its location at the heart of the city.

2
1 | 3

1. *Shadows under the El on East 43rd Street west of Third Avenue about 1910.*
2. *Laundry hanging from converted brownstones about 1900.*
3. *839 Second Avenue at 45th Street about 1910.*

EX-LAX
FOR CONSTIPATION
PRESCRIPTION PHARMACY
SECOND AVE. PHARMACY
837
FARMACIA ITALIANA
CHEMICALS

The Willow Tree in Turtle Bay Gardens.

THE NEW RESIDENTIAL AREA.

AT THE END of the First World War, the midtown East River area had reached its lowest state, but history was to repeat itself once more. As described by Mildred Adams in "Again the City Seeks Its Rivers" (*New York Times Magazine*—1929): although the "mansions of one age became the slums of another," yet "if one waits long enough neighborhoods may return to their original destinies." Shortly after the war the trend set in and the residential character of the neighborhood began to improve markedly. These changes were also aptly referred to by Miss Adams: "too long had the land been buried under gravel dumps and coal bunkers. Turtle Cove, Beekman Place, the lovely triangle crowned by the old Gracie Mansion, held sleeping beauties which were due for a strenuous awakening."[10] First changes came in the form of rediscovery by knowledgeable people, the purchase of old brownstones and their subsequent remodeling. One of the least broken up blocks was the one bounded by 48th and 49th Streets and Second and Third Avenues. It was here in 1919 and 1920 that Mrs. Walton Martin conceived of using a series of houses to enclose a community garden on which all the houses would abut. Inspired by similar group housing designs in France and Italy where she had lived, Mrs. Martin sought out with great care twenty such houses. Ten faced north on 49th Street and ten south on 48th Street—each, therefore, having adjoining back yards. Six feet of land was taken from the rear of each lot to form a central path and common garden. The garden of each house was then arranged for individual privacy by means of low walls and landscaping. Trees were, wherever possible, preserved. Among these was a certain willow which had grown on the site of a branch of the brook which had trickled through the area down towards Turtle Bay.

It was E. B. White of *The New Yorker* who, living in Turtle Bay Gardens, immortalized the willow tree in the closing paragraph of his classic, "Here is New York:"

A block or two west of the city of man in Turtle Bay there is an old willow tree that presides over an interior garden. It is a battered tree, long suffering and much climbed, held together by strands of bailing wire but beloved by those who know it. In a way it symbolizes the city: life under difficulties, growth against odds, sap-rise in the midst of concrete, and the steady reaching for the sun. Whenever I look at it nowadays, and feel the cold shadow of planes, I think: 'This must be saved, this particular thing, this very tree. If it were to go, all would go—this city, this mischievous and marvelous monument which not to look upon would be like death.'[11]

Mrs. Martin renovated the exteriors of the houses in a somewhat uniform design under the guidance of Clarence Dean, a noted architect. The old high stoop entrances were converted into "American basement" types. Kitchens were moved to the street side of the houses and the living rooms were designed to face out over the gardens. In the gardens a copy of the fountain at the entrance of the Villa de Medici was placed near the willow. The properties were called Turtle Bay Gardens—a name probably selected by Dr. Walton Martin who had assembled a magnificent collection of engravings, books and maps of early New York. The Martins themselves lived in a double house at 228 East 49th Street.

Since its inception, the garden community has attracted prominent figures in New York's cultural life. Among them have been Dorothy Thompson, Katherine Hepburn, Maxwell Perkins, Leopold Stokowski, Ernest Poole, Tyrone Power, J. P. McEvoy, Mary Martin, Judge Learned Hand, Ambassador Phillip C. Jessup, Walter Kilham, Frances Grimes, Michael Greer, Stephen Sondheim and Dr. Dallas Pratt who, along with the late John Judkyn, was a co-founder of the American Museum near Bath, England which portrays American life from 1680 to 1880.

At about the same time that Mrs. Martin established

1. *Living room in duplex apartment of Michael Greer overlooking Turtle Bay Gardens.*
2. *Dining room and* **3.** *living room in the home of Mrs. Walton Martin in 1960.*

1 | 3
2

Saul Steinberg's drawing looks behind a brownstone front.

Turtle Bay Gardens, other rundown sections of the East Side were likewise feeling the stirrings of change. To the north, Sutton Place, originally called Avenue A but renamed for Effingham B. Sutton, a merchant who had developed the area in the 80's, was the scene of much renovation, inspired to a large degree by Mrs. William K. Vanderbilt, Anne Morgan (daughter of J. P. Morgan), Kermit Roosevelt (son of Theodore), Elizabeth Marbury (the prominent decorator) and Elsie de Wolfe.

Eventually the private house gave way to massive apartments. Again in the words of Miss Adams, written in 1929:

Now the whole water-front from forty-second to eighty-ninth streets is in a state of pereptual upheaval. Huge apartment houses stagger their roofs according to zoning regulations and the steel, stone and concrete dreams of their architects. There are some gaps where title has been difficult or plans have struck a snag, but the tide of building moves as fast as capital and steam shovels can move it.[12]

The largest development was that of Tudor City, opened in 1928 at a cost of some $25,000,000, with its apartments advertised on a "walk to work" basis. More than one hundred houses were acquired in 1925 by the Fred F. French development interests. These were demolished and in their place was erected a series of large apartment houses integrated as something of a city within a city. The Tudor style of architecture was used with its gables, stained glass window effects and flamboyant Gothic doorways. The original group had twelve buildings with three thousand apartments and six hundred hotel rooms capable of lodging seven thousand five hundred people. It occupied four city blocks between 40th and 43rd Street between First and Second Avenues. The community now has its own post office and publishes a monthly magazine, has two landscaped private parks and a children's playground. Curiously enough Tudor City Plaza, from 41st to 43rd Streets built above busy 42nd Street, is one of the quietest places in town. Not surprisingly, because of the then existing slaughterhouses on First Avenue, the living rooms of Tudor City were built facing the west and only the back corridors faced the River.

The apartment at 865 First Avenue was built about the same time. It was here that Thomas Wolfe lived in 1936 in an apartment on the fourteenth floor. He considered it "a fine place" with "about three sticks of dilapidated furniture, but one of the coolest places and one of the most wonderful views of New York." He described the East River as it then was: "a river which is busy at almost every moment of the day with its wonderful and thrilling traffic of boats, great and small: the busy tugs, the great barges, freighters and ships."[13]

In 1921, Turtle Bay Music School was established on East 52nd Street. Later it was used by the famed Desoff Choir for rehearsal. 1926 saw the erection of the Biblical Seminary on 49th Street when it moved from its previous location on Lexington Avenue. On 44th Street, the Beaux Arts Apartments and Hotel were built in 1929 and thought to be avant garde in their design by Raymond Howe. Because the apartments were considered so far off the beaten track, the management ran a bus shuttle to Grand Central Station and another to Rockefeller Center.

The old Beekman Hill atmosphere had been reasonably well preserved, but here, too, old houses were renovated or reconstructed. Apartments with terraces and gardens were built and through the decades Beekman Place remained one of the finest residential streets in the city. In 1929, Beekman Towers Hotel was completed. The same year witnessed the building of One Beekman Place—one of the most luxurious apartments of the time in New York, notwithstanding that its southern exposure overlooked one of the most dilapidated areas of the city.

Among the many well-known residents of Beekman Hill have been members of the Rockefeller family, Ethel Barrymore, Katherine Cornell, Irving Berlin, James Forrestal, and many prominent theatrical figures.

Hanley Hennock, a mural painter who has lived in Beekman Hill for over 43 years, has recalled these days:

In 1923 my sister and I bought 32 Beekman Place

the middle house of three built on a lot 100 ft. by 25 ft. facing on Beekman Place. The one to the right of ours was said to have been bought by David Belasco for his mistress. When the north end at 51st was built up the residents started a private bus to Broadway. Beekman Place then was cobbled with grass growing between the cobbles. First Avenue at that time was also cobbled with a Toonerville Trolley not more than 15 ft. long. . . .

At that time most of the houses had colonial small pane windows and on Christmas Eve a candle was placed in each pane and the local old ladies and gentlemen sang Christmas carols.

The neighborhood then was largely theatrical. Gilbert Seldes and his wife, just married, lived in our lower two floors. Carl Van Vechten used Beekman Place as the locale for one of his novels. The Fawcetts, both well known theatrically, lived in a house standing where No. 20 now is. Margalo Gilmore, her sister and her mother lived with the Fawcetts, I believe, and Percy Haswell, quite famous at the time and my favorite actress, also did. Patricia Collinge and her husband lived on 51st Street and Beekman Place. The Barrymores lived on the river side. Later, Katherine Cornell and Guthrie McClintic bought a house on the river side and Alfred Lunt and Lynn Fontanne lived on the northeast corner of 50th and Beekman. Helen Hokinson, the great cartoonist of dowager ladies of The New Yorker *also lived here.*

You may remember the famous Titterton murder case in 1936. Mrs. Titterton lived on the 2nd floor of what had been the Fawcett's house and was murdered there. The police came up with many strange clues. They knew that Mrs. Titterton was a friend of Frederick and Charles Jackson, the latter of "Lost Weekend" fame, and that Everett Linsley had met Mrs. Titterton with them at a restaurant so the three were questioned for hours. The police later found a string or cord used in upholstery and so traced the murder to a young man who had come in to upholster a chair.

When the house at the northeast corner of 51st Street and Beekman was done over, the new owner claimed that Nathan Hale had met his end there. A large mural was painted on the outside with Hale against the wall facing a firing squad! The house was so badly done over that people moved in one week and out every time the plaster fell. Hale House, as it was called, became known as 'Hale and Farewell House.' It has since been entirely done over.

Of strange stops in the neighborhood my favorite where I always bought fish was on Second Avenue between 48th and 49th Streets and where the man also sold live birds of all kinds—a combination you could not find any other place.

During the first World's Fair there was a regular boat service from 49th Street to Flushing Meadow which left from an old pier which is still there across the drive.

Balconies on Beekman Place, 1965.

Seven years after the Titterton murder, Beekman Hill became the scene of another equally famous case when the body of young Patricia Burton Lonergan, a wealthy heiress, was found sprawled across her antique Second Empire bed in her luxurious apartment on East 51st Street. The police traced this murder to her estranged husband and he eventually was convicted.

Changes also took place in the 1920's and 1930's in the upper 40's. On East 48th Street two new apartment houses were erected, and in the block between 47th and 48th Streets on the west side of Third Avenue a large apartment building appeared with a pleasant courtyard. In 1929, the midtown Hospital on 49th Street was completed.

During those years, too, various individual houses attained prominence. One of the best known was the house at 225–227 East 49th Street, built in 1926 by Efrem Zimbalist, the violinist, and where he and his wife, Alma Gluck, the celebrated opera star, and her daughter Marcia Davenport—the novelist, lived for several years. The Zimbalist house had a soundproof studio. Henry Luce of *Time-Life* also lived there. In later years (1957 to 1960), the former glories of this mansion were to be forgotten when the house was used as the 17th Police Precinct Station House. All of its paneled walls and artistic interior were torn out to give way to iron stairways and the pea green decor so typical of municipal institutions.

Other houses of note built or reconstructed at this time were the house of William Lescaze, the noted architect, at 211 East 48th Street, built in 1934, characterized by the use of glass bricks and having one of the first home air conditioning systems; the Michael Hare house at 212 East 49th Street; and the Morris Sanders house at 219 East 49th Street, both of which, along with the Lescaze house, were considered at the time to be daringly advanced.

In the 1930's and '40's New York was now becoming increasingly congested. Third Avenue, Second Avenue and First Avenue had always been major arteries along the east side, but the elevated railroad pillars effectively disqualified the first two of these from automobile traffic. It was soon realized that bold traffic measures would be required. As a part of the New York circular highway, the East River Drive was first begun in the late '30's. At first a four-lane highway running north and south, it was completed with considerable rebuilding as an effective arterial link by the end of World War II. It was renamed for President Franklin D. Roosevelt who had died in 1945. A good part of the fill under the roadway of the FDR Drive came across the Atlantic as ballast in American ships returning from Great Britain during World War II loaded with the rubble of London blitzes.

East 49th Street showing former Zimbalist house and Biblical Seminary.

209

1 | **3**
2 |

1. *Air view of Tudor City about 1935. The Second Avenue El was still running and brownstones with awnings lined parts of the streets.*

2. *East River Drive in front of Beekman Hill in early forties.*

3. *East River front from 35th Street to 55th Street in the early thirties showing Beekman Hill in the center and slaughterhouses on the present United Nations site to the left. Welfare Island, formerly Blackwell's Island, is in the foreground.*

In 1944, a group of tenements located in an L-shaped courtyard at 211 East 49th Street was remodeled and developed by the noted designer James Amster into a complex of offices, studios and apartments. At one time the terminal of the Boston Stage Coach line and site of Isamu Noguchi's studio (the world-renowned modern sculptor), this courtyard is aptly described as a "garden oasis" and one of the most beautiful small enclosures in the city. The architect was Harold Sterner. The east boundary of the Amster Yard garden is set off by a large mirror which gives the illusion of doubling the garden area.

The demolition of the Second Avenue El in 1942 signaled the beginning of the end of the tenement areas. Its effect did not show until after World War II when the current building boom started. Many, if not most, of the old tenement walk-ups have now been replaced by large apartments along Second Avenue and in the side streets from 44th Street up into the 50's and well beyond. Fourteen new apartment houses have been erected between East 44th and East 49th Streets in six years, where not a single apartment building had been built in the three previous decades.

Many old brownstones which remained have been refaced and have had their interiors rebuilt along the lines of the Turtle Bay Garden houses. Treeless streets have now become well planted and the old slabs of concrete between houses and sidewalks have, in many cases, been replaced by bushes, shrubs and flowers. Before World War II, parts of the Turtle Bay area had been used in the films as the location for "Dead End." In 1962, houses on 49th Street, which has passed through roominghouse days, had now acquired sufficient dignity to serve as scenes of the home of a mythological United States Senator in the film "Manchurian Candidate."

It was also during these postwar years that most of the second-hand shops in the area metamorphosed into antique shops. This development was followed by the influx of a large number of decorators and artists. Rents were low and the shadows of the Third Avenue El, which did not come down until 1956, preserved to Third Avenue an antique character all its own. Moreover, apart from the El, there was little traffic so that professional decorators and elderly little ladies could wander about. One could usually park a car or station wagon to remove a treasured purchase. There was one particular corner on 51st Street with a charming inside alley surrounded by little antique shops. This was known as Ardlea Court. Curiously, it was developed at the end of the 19th Century by none other than Richard Croker who had reigned over Tammany Hall from 1886 to 1901, more familiarly known as "Boss" Croker. Croker had been in London and was impressed by the Dickens-like quality of many areas of the city. Upon his return, he thought it well to reproduce a spot of Old London right under the shadow of the El. Croker's Ardlea Court died almost simultaneously with the El. Its site is now the Girl Scout building. One of the more modest antique shops was run by Celestino Fontana on 49th Street on the site of the present United States Plywood Building. He was described by Meyer Berger in 1952:[14]

Celestino Fontana is the St. Francis of East Forty-ninth Street. For some twelve years now, the birds in the block between Third and Second Avenues have fed from his generous hands. He has healed the injured in neighborhood pigeon flocks, has reared their orphaned young.

Celestino is a bulky, gray-haired fellow. As a child in Crescentino near the Cottian Alps he tended wounded wild things, then freed them. At 12, he went into the world and much later, as maître d'hotel on the Riviera, in London, in Boston and in New York, came to serve royalty.

Then he opened his little antique shop at 202 East Forty-ninth Street. He filled it with odds and ends from the homes of rich folk he had met. But the birds were really his prime interest. They run Celestino. They run the shop.

Each night before he locks the dusty little shop, Celestino goes outside and spreads wholewheat bread crumbs close to the walls beside his place. He blankets Pop and Louie, his two hoary parrots, in their cages, then retires to the rear.

When morning light comes into Forty-ninth Street the pigeons fly down from Manny Wolf's roof

1. *Amster Yard showing James Amster's house and* 2. *his living room.*

across the street. They assail the shop's window. They peck at it with their beaks. Forty or fifty huddle expectantly in the stone doorway.

Then Celestino comes out and they cover him. One day, he remembers, some 400 swooped from near-by roofs and actually bore him to the flagstones. He feeds them four to six loaves of bread, hemp seed, prepared bird foods.

'Ho!' he trumpets. 'Do they know Celestino? But watch them one day. They embrace Celestino. They knock him down for love of him.'

Rich customers bring sick birds to the shop. The stout shopkeeper makes splints for them with cigar-box wood and adhesive tape. He puts them in one of the five enormous cages. He says, 'Pop and Louie, they would tear these other ones apart. They even scold the customers.'

They do, too. They have free run of the shop, and a stranger is often startled by some acid comment from the top of a red plush screen or the cornice of a gold-and-pink curio chest. Old Louie, gray-lidded, sleepily says, 'Get out! Get 'em out!" It isn't good for trade, but somehow it delights Celestino.

When night comes in East Forty-ninth Celestino puts on a single, sickly yellow light, straps his big accordion to his shoulders and, with a cigar stump tight in his teeth, serenades Pop and Louie with ancient Italian folk tunes. The birds raucously sing them.

Passers-by who do not know Celestino's shop but come suddenly upon it are entranced by the night scene—the big accordionist, the swooping birds, the big cages, the dusty window, the neglected silver, glass and enamelware all cast in thin yellow light. It is Dickens in low key in a New York side street.

The old Turtle Bay area is today the home of well-known persons from every walk of life, but it retains a special attraction for people associated with the worlds of literature, the theatre and the arts. In addition to those whose names have already been noted, residents have included representatives of the theater such as Burgess Meredith, Cornelia Otis Skinner, Irving Berlin, Billy Rose, Melvyn Douglas, Ralph Bellamy, Frederic March, Humphrey Bogart, Stephen Sondheim, Garson Kanin and his wife Ruth Gordon, Samuel Taylor, Brian Aherne, Greta Garbo; such representatives of the world of literature as Cornelius Ryan, Henry M. Robinson and Eugene Reynal; some of the figures from the art world have been Henry Koehler, Emily Genauer, Thomas Hess, Alice Winchester, Kay Reynal and Saul Steinberg; fashion designers such as Norman Norell and architects like Ieoh Ming Pei, the newly chosen architect of the John F. Kennedy Memorial Library.

Beekman Place is the home of Mary Lasker, the widow of the noted philanthropist, Albert D. Lasker, and who has contributed so much to the beautification of New York. Not content with planting tulips and chrysanthemums in the spring along Beekman Place and a goodly number of trees along several blocks of 50th Street, it was Mrs. Lasker who in 1956 demonstrated to the city fathers that Park Avenue could more fully deserve its name by the planting of trees for 22 blocks. As if this were not enough, Mary Lasker and her family then presented flowering cherry trees for the United Nations Garden along with 40,000 daffodil bulbs.

The unofficial "mayor of First Avenue" is Frank De Stasio who was born nearly seventy years ago on 48th Street. In his youth he cut wood for Ethel Barrymore and for the past thirty years he has maintained a barber shop on First Avenue near the United Nations with a host of celebrities as patrons, including most of the best known residents, as well as Dag Hammarskjöld, Henry Cabot Lodge and Billy Graham.

The last few years have witnessed the development of a neighborhood spirit. The Turtle Bay Association, formed in 1957, is designed to preserve the residential character of the upper forties and lower fifties and to help residents know each other better. As a memorial to Charlotte Hunnewell Martin, a fund has been established to defray the costs of new trees and shrubs in the streets. Representatives of the Association make it a point to appear before the City Board and at City Hall to give renewed emphasis to the importance of the individual and as well as the community in the face of the ever-growing mechanization of life.

The End of the Brownstone. *A water color by Polly Jackson.*

1

THE UNITED NATIONS COMMUNITY.

DURING 1946 THE United Nations had considered a variety of proposals for its eventual location. The choice seemed to favor settling down in Westchester or Connecticut when on December 11, 1946 John D. Rockefeller, Jr. offered $8,500,000 to acquire an available site on the East River as a permanent home for the world organization. The proposed area was occupied by old abattoirs, breweries and cold storage bins located along the River and First Avenue between 42nd and 48th Streets. The parcels for this plot had been assembled by a well-known real estate syndicate headed by William Zeckendorf originally for use as a private development. The Rockefeller offer was promptly accepted and Congress, in what must have been one of the most rapid passages of legislation, enacted a special statute exempting the Rockefeller gift from the normal gift tax. The City agreed to contribute certain adjacent properties including water front rights along the East River.

While the United Nations buildings were under construction in 1947, Zeckendorf offered plans for a wide concourse approach to the area to be built without cost to the City or the United Nations. The plan as announced called for condemnation of all the blocks between 46th Street and 49th Street from First to Third Avenues and the complete demolition of the Turtle Bay Gardens as well as of all the other renovated houses which would have had to be abandoned. Vigorous opposition promptly developed. The plan was soon laid to rest at a memorable hearing before the City Board of Estimate which was characterized in the press as a session filled with "verbal pyrotechnics" and the "most heated personal exchanges the Board has witnessed in recent years." After Zeckendorf leveled charges at the then Mayor O'Dwyer of "rump session," "usurpation of power" and "abdication of responsibility," he also charged Commissioner Robert Moses with "damnable lies." Zeckendorf was ordered out of the meeting by the Mayor and the Board.

Turtle Bay Gardens and other emerging areas were saved and, as an approach to the United Nations, the City adopted a Moses plan for widening 47th Street between First and Second Avenues, and building the tunnel under First Avenue for through traffic leaving the Plaza above the tunnel.

Work was quickly begun and the old buildings in the area were razed. In their place was erected a magnificent group of buildings in well landscaped surroundings. Outstanding is the tall glass and marble Secretariat which dominates the East River landscape. Adjacent to it is the General Assembly building with its great meeting hall. On the River side is a series of conference chambers. Along the 42nd Street side is a new library building completed in 1963.

1. *The United Nations permanent headquarters in 1962.*
2. *"Single Form"—memorial sculpture for the late Dag Hammarskjöld.*

United Nations site in 1946 taken from Tudor City.

Rejected East Side development conceived by William Zeckendorf.

The rising Secretariat building in July (below) and September, 1949.

CRAWFORD

Teakwood statue symbolizing Mankind and Hope in Trusteeship Council Chamber donated by Denmark.

Approximately $67,000,000 has been spent for the building program at the United Nations. The buildings were designed by W. K. Harrison and Max Abramowitz working along with the leading architects of the world including France's Le Corbuisier, Brazil's Oscar Niemeyer, Russia's Nikolai Bassow and Sweden's Sven Markelius.

The Secretariat building was completed in 1950. It rises 505 feet above street level. Notable in the foyer is a stained glass window designed and painted by France's Marc Chagall. The fountain in the Plaza in front of the building is a gift from the school children of the United States. This is also the site of a large abstract sculpture by England's Barbara Hepworth which, along with the Chagall window, is a memorial to Dag Hammarskjöld, the late Secretary General who died in a plane crash in Central Africa in 1961. An interesting design exists on the bottom of the pool created by alternating bands of crushed white marble and black stone. Between the Secretariat building and the Conference building is a Japanese pagoda. Facing United Nations Plaza is a long arc on which the flags of all the nations are flown.

In 1952 the General Assembly was completed. Its entrance is marked by an extraordinary main lobby with windows along the East River. Underneath the lobby is the United Nations book shop, a post office, gift center and coffee shop.

The General Assembly chamber itself is remarkable for its almost perfect acoustics. The side walls are decorated with murals by the famous French artist, Fernand Leger and one of his pupils. In the Assembly Building are also two enormous murals by Candido Portinari of Brazil.

The conference area which, like the General Assembly, is on a low level contains three council chambers: the Economic and Social Council, the Trusteeship Council and the Security Council. Throughout the conference area, there are a number of distinguished murals and furnishings noteworthy among which is the statue of a child with upraised arms carved from Teakwood by Henrik Starcke, a Danish sculptor, symbolizing Mankind and Hope. Other murals have been contributed by the Norwegian Per Krohg and the Dominican artist, Jose Vela Zanetti. In the Conference building can also be found the great tapestry made in Bruges, Belgium. The library, now named for Dag Hammarskjöld, was completed in 1962.

In the gardens surrounding the buildings can be seen two beautiful statues, one representing a woman rider on a horse symbolic of peace presented by Yugoslavia and sculptured by Antun Augustincic, and the other representing Man turning his sword into a plow presented by the Soviet Union.

Stained glass memorial to Dag Hammarskjöld and the fifteen others who died with him in 1961 plane crash depicts Peace and Man. Located in Secretariat lobby, it was donated by U.N. staff members.

Nickel-plated doors at entrance to United Nations donated by the Canadian government in 1952.

"Let Us Beat Swords Into Ploughshares." Statue given the United Nations by the Soviet Union.

1. *Japanese Peace Bell donated in 1954 to the United Nations.*

2. *Bronze equestrian statue symbolizing Peace donated by Yugoslavia in 1954.*

3. *Foucault Pendulum, donated by the Netherlands, in lobby of the General Assembly. The 200-pound, gold-plated sphere is held by a stainless steel wire allowing it to swing freely in any plane directly over the raised metal ring which contains an electric magnet in the center. The sphere swings continuously as a pendulum, its plane shifting slowly in a clockwise direction. As in the original experiment of Jean Bernard Leon Foucault in 1851, it offers visual proof of the earth's rotation. A complete cycle takes about 36 hours and 45 minutes.*

With the development of the United Nations Plaza came extensive changes on First Avenue.

Among the new buildings associated with the Plaza is the United States Mission designed by Kily and Cruzer, Kahn and Jacks with its delightful courtyard dedicated by President Eisenhower in 1961. Also notable are the Herbert Hoover building for Boys Clubs, the Institute of International Education, the Carnegie Endowment for International Center and the United Engineering Center housing the national offices of numerous professional engineering societies completed in 1961. The American Institute of Physics is on 45th Street between the U.N. Plaza and Second Avenue.

The semi-official activities along the United Nations Plaza are now being extended south to 42nd Street where the new Ford Foundation Building between First and Second Avenues on the site of the former Grand Central Hospital, and adjacent to Tudor City, promises to be a landmark in New York office building architecture. It is the work of associates of the late Eero Saarinen: Joseph N. Lacy, John Dinkehloo and Kevin Roche. Designed as an open-sided square with an L-shaped office building, it will have an interior skylit court containing a 100-foot garden with trees and natural rock. Three-quarters of the south side of the building and two-fifths of the east side will consist of sheer glass rising 130 feet. Writing in *The New York Times,* these plans were described by the *Times* architect critic, Ada Louise Huxtable.[15]

The design is surprisingly reminiscent of a popular kind of Victorian business building of the late 19th century where elaborately balconied office floor surrounded a full-height, skylit court. These buildings are being destroyed across the country as obsolete.

* * *

This is . . . an object lesson in the possibilities opened by fresh thought and a creative approach to the city's most important commercial building problem: the provision of ample and impressive headquarters for large corporations or equivalent organizations, in structures that have some civic conscience as well.

This building promises to achieve the rather remarkable feat of living comfortably with neighboring styles that range from hasty-pudding-commercial to mock-neo-Tudor. It is a small addition to a big town, in New York's way of measuring landmarks by size, but it is a large potential dose of design quality in a city that matches its extraordinary vitality with the deadliness of its building cliches.

1. *Architectural model of the Ford Foundation Building.*
2. *United Engineering Center houses major American engineering societies and the most comprehensive engineering library in the world.*

Among the relatively few commercial enterprises in the area is the IBM World Trade Center on the Plaza at 47th Street. To the north of the United Nations there will be found in the course of erection what has been described as the largest combination office and luxury apartment building. This project covers a full city block between 48th and 49th Street from the East River Drive to the United Nations Plaza. It will be marked by twin towers with a height of 38 stories rising through a six-story office building and housing 334 co-operative apartments. Designers of the United Nations Plaza Building, as it is to be called, are the firm of Harrison & Abramovitz.

The area around the United Nations Plaza harbors a number of religious institutions which have been specifically developed to minister to the U.N. community along with local residents. At 44th Street is a new Church Center of the United Nations designed by William Lescaze with a 12-story tower sheathed in bronze and glass and a beautiful chapel of marble and mahogany colored wood, backed by a massive stained-glass window by Henry L. Willet symbolizing man's struggle for peace and brotherhood. Along 47th Street the old Catholic Church of the Holy Family, which had been converted from a brewery stable prior to the First World War, has now been completely renovated and boasts a 142-foot bell tower. The church property includes a rectory, an information center and a garden. The architecture (George J. Sole, architect) is contemporary and harmonizes with the new buildings in the area. The windows and murals by Jordi Bonet, a Catalan, portray refugees of all countries and eras led by the Holy Family in the flight into Egypt.

Not far away will be a new Jewish Center on 51st Street near Second Avenue which will include a sanctuary, library, research facilities and a museum. At Second Avenue and East 43rd Street, the Episcopal Church has erected a trim new office building to serve as its general headquarters. This building contains the Chapel of Christ the Lord with a 13-foot high Celtic Cross and a beautiful tapestry designed by Allen Porter and made in Germany. The abstract windows are the work of Gabriel Loire of Chartres.

On 42nd Street the Presbyterian Church of the Covenant still stands, its approaches clipped over the years by the widening of 42nd Street, but still remaining as a community church in the Tudor City area.

On 48th Street near Second Avenue stands Quaker House, the residence of the executive director in charge of Quaker interests in the United Nations. The House has been used to entertain many delegates to the U.N., for discussions of world problems and for the great philanthropic work of the American Friends Service Committee.

Since establishment of the U.N. in Turtle Bay, the land granted in 1639 by Dutch Governor William Kieft to Holmes and Hall has been visited by every President of the United States, practically every world monarch and by every world statesman who would have the least claim to such designation.

Apartment house coming down to make way for United Nations Plaza Building going up.

Aluminum-sheathed twin towers of United Nations Plaza Building, sponsored by Alcoa Plaza Associates, under construction in 1964. In the foreground, a hydrofoil used for World's Fair transportation.

Church of the Holy Family on East 47th Street. Exterior is gray granite with an aluminum bell tower.

Church Center at the United Nations, sheathed in bronze and glass, completed in 1963 by the Methodist Church.

1 | 2

1. *The Episcopal Church Center at 43rd Street and Second Avenue (1964).*
2. *Chapel of Christ the Lord in Episcopal Church Center.*

SAVILE'S ROW OF OFFICE TOWERS.

THE LAST El train made its final run on May 12, 1955. A year later the last pillar supporting the tracks was removed, Third Avenue was widened, trees were planted and fluorescent street lighting was installed. All of this touched off a building explosion. The next seven years were to witness the largest number of commercial office buildings to be erected in such a small portion of one avenue—41st Street to 52nd Street, roughly marking the western fringes of the old Turtle Bay grants of 1639 and 1676. Just as in the case of the residential renewal, it was inevitable that a business area so close to Grand Central Station would boil over with business activity once the old El disappeared.

And so it was that the old brownstones laced with fire escapes were gradually torn down, plots were assembled and new commercial towers sprang up on each side of the avenue. The old pawnshops were replaced by banks and brokerage houses; delicatessens disappeared one by one, and the residents began to patronize the new supermarkets along Second Avenue. Hardware stores and paint shops moved elsewhere or went out of business. One of the last old-timers was the Richardson & Dutt Lumberyard which closed in 1962, for many years the mecca of the do-it-yourself enthusiasts. Only there could one find the moldings, panels and decorative lumber which were unique in their variety and artistic lines. On this site stands the United States Plywood building.

Nor was the building spree confined to Third Avenue. Activity extends to both sides of East 42nd Street toward the River and to many of the side streets in the lower 40's. Even before World War II, East 42nd Street was the site of one of the finest commercial office buildings in America. Indeed the Daily News building (John Mead Howells and Raymond Hood, architects) erected in 1930 was later to receive an award from the Municipal Arts Society and the Society of Architectural Historians for "originality in design and its influence on later work." In the lobby of the News building, there is a large world globe rotating under a superbly executed dome. In 1958 the attractive News annex was completed at the Second Avenue corner with its small, pleasant WPIX Plaza.

The News building was the pioneer. There were few other buildings of note either on Third Avenue or at the eastern end of 42nd Street until 1951 when the Chrysler annex at 666 Third Avenue was built even while the Third Avenue El was still in full operation. The real boom began with the erection of the Socony Mobil building in 1956 (Harrison & Abramowitz, architects) with its huge 1,300,000 square feet of office space.

The new skyscrapers built after World War II reflect the changes which have taken place since the pre-war period when the competitive feature of commercial building was a question of height. The days of the Chrysler and Empire State buildings are probably over because high building costs and more stringent zoning have dictated buildings from twenty to forty stories.

Yet the stark mechanical quality of modern office buildings, once described as "upright coffins," has been such that builders and architects have sought to inject some artistic conceptions to bring them a touch of human warmth. In the late 1950's, this "shotgun wedding of art and architecture," to use the phrase of Emily Genauer, art critic for *The New York Herald Tribune* and herself a Turtle Bay resident, became increasingly evident in the new buildings which were being erected on the site of the old Turtle Bay Farm. These works generally took the form of murals or abstract sculptures. Reactions have been as varied as there are critics, but whatever may be one's evaluation of a particular work, one can only hope that in some form at least there may be an integration of art and architecture so as to humanize, even in some small way, the bleak materialism of the new generation of skyscrapers.

1. *Looking north at 41st Street and Third Avenue. Continental Can Building at right center erected in 1962.*

1 | 2

1. *Third Avenue Elevated looking north from 34th Street just before it came down. Chrysler Building East is to right of the Chrysler Building.*

2. *New York Daily News Building built in 1930 with News Annex at left completed in 1958.*

DAILY
NEWS
75°
WPIX
11

HOTEL
LINCOLN
TUNNEL

Across First Avenue is a new building with a façade of glass and bronze-toned aluminum at 300 East 42nd Street (William Lescaze, architect). Across from the new Ford Foundation building is the Pfizer World Headquarters (Leonard—Colangelo—Peters, architects—1960) with an interesting mural (Nikos Bell-Jon) depicting in vivid and ever changing colors some of the high spots of the history of medicine, a description of which is made available to the viewer merely by picking up a telephone and listening to the recorded story. Near the Pfizer building is the R.E.A. (Railway Express Agency) Building (remodeled by Fred Safron, architect) with a pleasant lobby mural by F. Bensagne entitled "Space and Movement."

Proceeding northward on Third Avenue from 41st Street at the southern fringe of old Turtle Bay Farm, there is the Continental Can building (633 Third Avenue), remarkable perhaps because of the interesting use of bricks, aluminum and glass (Harrison & Abramowitz, architects—1962). Across the street is the Lorillard building at 200 East 42nd Street on the corner of Third Avenue with an arresting abstract fountain in the lobby entitled "Moon City" by H. Jack Sharman and Alfred Chas. Stern and an unusual exterior abstract sculpture entitled "Windward" by Jan Peter Stern.

North of 42nd Street is 201 East 42nd Street and the Diamond National Building lobby (Emery Roth & Sons, architects); 711 Third Avenue (William Lescaze, architect—1956) has a pleasing design and a fine mosaic by Hans Hofmann in the lobby. Of particular note is the sculpture *Continuum* by Jose de Rivera which has the distinction of having been taken down from the building and exhibited at Whitney Museum in 1959.

One of the most pleasing and distinctive buildings is the Harcourt Brace & World building at 757 Third Avenue (Emery Roth & Sons, architects) with its attractive colonnade and interior mosaics. The ground floor contains a fascinating book shop designed by Clothiel Woodward Smith which represents a new concept in the merchandising of reading materials.

Across the street are the General Telephone Building at 730 and the 750 Third Avenue Building located at 46th Street, the scene of the old Civil War riots in 1863. These buildings—almost twins—are somewhat heavy and ponderous to behold, but the interior of 750 is graced by some fine abstract bronze sculptures by David Hare (1958). The central one (40 by 15 feet) is attached to a concave wall and is flanked by two corridor panels approximately 30 by 10 feet each.

The United States Plywood building (William Lescaze, architect) at 49th Street lend grace and dignity to the avenue by virtue of its plaza and arcade passages and its being set back from the street line. It has a fine 18-foot architectural sculpture *Contra Punto* by Beverly Pepper consisting of rounded forms which contrast with the straight perpendiculars of the building.

So it has come to pass that in the last ten years, Third Avenue has been transformed from a gloomy cobblestone street to a Savile's Row of office towers and several cases of unusually high architectural merit now housing the head offices of some of the most prominent corporate enterprises in the U.S.

1. *300 E. 42nd Street with Hotel Tudor in background.*
2. *Bronze sculpture by David Hare at 750 Third Avenue.*

CAFETERIA
AUTOMAT

1 | 2

1. *Lorillard Building completed in 1958. On the right is a corner of the Socony Mobil Building.*

2. *201 East 42nd Street (artist's rendering, 1964).*

1 | 2

1. *Under the El at Third Avenue and 46th Street looking south. Former site of old cottages on Third Avenue and present site of the Diamond National Building.*
2. *Diamond National Building at Third Avenue and 46th Street.*

REILLY
TYPO
GRAMERCY
MOVING
STORAGE

1 | 2

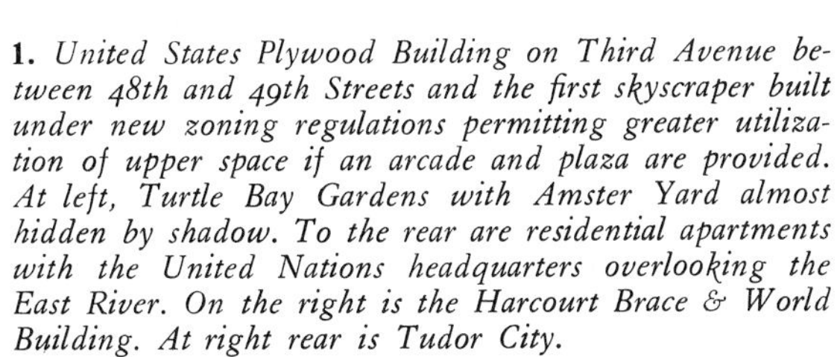

1. *United States Plywood Building on Third Avenue between 48th and 49th Streets and the first skyscraper built under new zoning regulations permitting greater utilization of upper space if an arcade and plaza are provided. At left, Turtle Bay Gardens with Amster Yard almost hidden by shadow. To the rear are residential apartments with the United Nations headquarters overlooking the East River. On the right is the Harcourt Brace & World Building. At right rear is Tudor City.*

2. *"Contra Punto," 18-foot architectural sculpture at entrance to United States Plywood Building by Beverly Pepper.*

Quelques-unes de nos Spécialités

Le CAFÉ CHAMBORD offre à sa clientèle, au Déjeuner et au Dîner, une sélection variée des plus fameux plats Provinciaux de France.

Pâté de Foie Gras, Importation CHAMBORD

La Timbale de Pintadon Garnie au Foie Gras
et Truffes Importés

Le Petit Coq Préparé Belle Vue
avec toute sa Garniture

Le Grenadin de Veau cuit en Casserole
Cordon Bleu

La Noix de Veau Sautée avec toute sa Garniture
Tante Louise

La Côte d'Agneau Anglaise Double
Grillée comme à Londres

Le Tournedos de Choix, Délice Belle Adrienne

Les Rognons de Veau Flambés au Cognac et Armagnac
Maître Chauveron

Le Chapon de Choix Sauté
au Vieux Vin Rouge Importé

L'Entrecôte à la Broche à la Vraie Mode Paloise

Les Filets de Caneton au Fruit de Floride
et au Grand Marnier Importé

Le Chapon de luxe Grillé aux Champignons
et Beurre demi-Glace

Le Poulet Reine Entier, en Casserole
Champ d'Oisel

La Partie du Baron d'Agneau au Gratin
et aux Champignons

Baba au Rhum
Pêches au Brandy
Parfait aux Liqueurs

Baked Alaska
Crêpes Suzette
Cerises Jubilée

Some of our Specialities

CAFÉ CHAMBORD presents to its patrons, for Lunch and Dinner, a varied selection of the most famous dishes from the Provinces of France.

Pâté de Foie Gras, Importation CHAMBORD

Le Coq de Choix à la Crème et au Foie Gras
Flambé au Cognac

Le Buisson de Grenouilles de Choix
Préparation Belle Provence

Le Shad Roe du Delaware Gratiné des Connaisseurs

La Croustade de Homard Farcie à Notre Manière

Les Filets de Pompanos au Vin Blanc
Glacés Bon Seigneur

Le Roi des Rochers, Grillé au Beurre Fin des Vignerons

La Belle Truite de Ruisseau aux Raisins
et Glacée au Vin Blanc

Les Filets de Sea Bass au Vin Blanc Importé
et Glacés Marguery

Le Roi des Rochers Flambé au Cognac
comme en Bretagne

L'Habitant des Rochers Flambé à l'Absinthe
Délices des Connaisseurs

Le Tendre Lapereau au Vin Vieux
en Marinade des Gourmets

La Noix des Ris de Veau, Braisée aux Marrons
et Cognac Importés

Le Pigeonneau en Cocotte aux Petits Pois Nouveaux
à la Française

Omelette Soufflée au Rhum
Soufflé Bénédictine

Soufflé Grand Marnier
Soufflé Chambord

Menus from Café Chambord.

EAT, DRINK AND BE MERRY.

THE REVEREND BURNABY'S description of Cato's Tavern and the turtle feasts of 1759 presaged a great tradition of epicurean achievement along old Turtle Bay. Cato's served its fine food until 1853, but as the rural atmosphere disappeared and the city expanded to the north, Third Avenue and Second Avenue became the site of a conglomeration of little Catos with swinging doors unequaled for density of population by any other area of New York. It has been said that there was a saloon with swinging doors on every corner. In the few cases where there was no saloon on the corner, thirst could be readily quenched in the middle of the block.

The advent of prohibition after the War sounded the death knell of the old saloon. In its place a number of speakeasies catered to the ever-present thirst not only of the local population but also that of patrons from other parts of the city who found comfort along Third Avenue. In the meantime, the low rents which persisted in the area attracted small restaurants operated by French, Italians, Greeks and Germans furnishing excellent meals at modest prices.

The repeal of prohibition in 1933 brought new interest to the pastimes of eating and drinking. Soon old saloons, now described as bars, reopened and these were run mostly by the Sons of Erin. Third Avenue became the traditional 19th hole for the St. Patrick's Day Parade. Of these bars, perhaps the best known is Costello's at 44th Street and Third Avenue which still has the old tradition of hospitality and boasts murals drawn on the wall by the noted author and cartoonist James Thurber depicting the unending wars between male and female. Costello's, which is frequented by newsmen and writers, was a favorite spot of Brendan Behan, Hemingway, H. L. Menken and Alexander Wollcott to mention but a few of its many famed patrons. Another favorite spot is to be found at McCarthy's on Second Avenue.

The neighborhood's reputation for alcoholic hospitality in the post prohibition days was such that much of the filming of "The Lost Weekend" took place on Third Avenue.

The temptation to write of gastronomy is difficult to resist, but the merits of Turtle Bay cuisine have been so fully described by writers and epicureans that there would be little to add. Restaurants come and go and their chefs and managers and menus change from year to year. But old-timers survive and these now proudly boast of a clientele as equally distinguished as their cooking.

One of the oldest restaurants carrying on today is Joe and Rose at Third Avenue and 45th Street, founded in 1915 and continuing its long patronage of actors from Richard Dix, Gloria Swanson and Rudolph Valentino to Frederic March, Ralph Bellamy and Perry Como.

The Palm, over on Second Avenue, like Joe and Rose, is surrounded by the new skyscrapers, but the owner does not intend to give up his brownstone. Founded in 1925, it was a favorite steak house of the late Toscanini and its walls carry drawings by celebrities in every walk of life.

Manny Wolf's, on 49th Street, moved up from Forsythe Street on the lower East Side in 1935 leaving behind memories of having catered to Diamond Jim Brady, Lillian Russell (who herself at one time lived at Second Avenue and 49th Street), Sarah Bernhardt, Mark Twain and Al Smith, but now caters to a new host of celebrities comfortably seated under some fine paintings by Cenic, Giordano and Madonnini.

The Pen and Pencil on 45th Street, properly called "Steak Row," was founded in 1935 by John Bruno who still checks its day to day operations. Bruno recalls that Anthony Eden one day was so pleased with his steak that he ordered twelve sent by air as a present to Winston Churchill in London. Bruno is also proud of his portrait of Dag Hammarskjöld which hangs over Hammarskjöld's favorite luncheon table, but he is apologetic about having kept Vice President Nixon waiting a half hour because the doorman merely told him that "Dick" was there thinking that it was unnecessary to further identify such a well-known customer. Adjoining the Pen

and Pencil is Pietro's established in 1934.
The Assembly Steak House on East 43rd Street is not an official eating spot for United Nations personnel, but it has assumed an important unofficial status. Its non-partisanship can be seen by the fact that the patronage of Ambassador Henry Cabot Lodge was followed by that of Adlai Stevenson. Because of its name, it frequently receives United Nations delegates who, being new to New York, ask a taxi to take them to the "Assembly" but end up at a restaurant rather than at the United Nations. Those fortunate enough to have come during the water shortage in New York in October 1963 would have received champagne as a courtesy substitute beverage with a note from the management regretting "any inconvenience" to the guest. Near the Assembly is Scoop with an equally distinguished and loyal clientele.
Possibly the best known of all restaurants of old Turtle Bay was Chambord which opened in 1936 and included among its patrons, to paraphrase Chaucer, figures of "every degree and condition." The renown of Chambord was world-wide. It was considered to be the most expensive restaurant in New York notwithstanding its location under the El. Its Founder, Roger Chauveron, has told the story:

"We opened at a time when everyone was broke," Mr. Chauveron reminisced, "and on Third Avenue! My proprietor told me I was crazy to open there in a pretty unfashionable neighborhood and that close to the elevated.
"We charged 75 cents for lunch and $1.75 for dinner, with a fine French chef and some of the best waiters in town. We were deluged with customers and so I started raising prices a nickel a week—it was the depression, you remember.
"Well, one day I discovered I had the most expensive restaurant in America: $20 for dinner for two which would be roughly $40 for two today. We also had more wines than any restaurant in New York—a cellar full of such vintages as 1891, 1896, 1897 and '99."[16]

Chambord moved away in 1963, but Turtle Bay can still boast of two of the newer luxurious restaurants in New York: Lutèce, which collects its patrons in a Parisian bus, opened its doors on 50th Street in 1961, offers a selection of over 300 French wines and is located in an old brownstone house with something of a Parisian front embellished with beautiful flowers; and, adjacent to it, The Leopard, an even more recent arrival, also housed in an old-world town house named by the proprietor after an ancestor, the Sicilian Prince of the same novel by de Lampedusa.
In these few blocks of New York can be found an infinite variety of eating places of every type and background and for all purses. There are old-time bars and grills, cafeterias for quick bites, espresso houses, little restaurants offering but a few selected dishes, well-known steak houses, cocktail lounges and night clubs offering a variety of entertainment, or what sometimes passes as such, "exclusive" establishments of great luxury which (to paraphrase J. P. Morgan's answer to an inquiry concerning the cost of a yacht) for one who must inquire about the price should not undertake to patronize. Some of these establishments reflect Victorian America, others are French bistros; some effect a "continental background," others are contemporary in style and some have little or no style at all.
Equally varied is the proffered cuisine: French, Italian, Belgian, German, English, Irish or Polish; Middle Eastern, Central Asian or Indian; Chinese—Mandarin or Cantonese; Philippine or Polynesian and back to Hawaii; or any number of varieties of American cooking.
And so it is that the tradition of *haute cuisine* begun by Cato over two hundred years ago still continues, but little could he have suspected that wining and dining would someday develop into one of the major activities of Turtle Bay.

Lutèce, a brownstone restaurant.

POSTSCRIPT.

The story of Turtle Bay reflects the vitality of New York and New Yorkers, their willingness to accept and welcome the *New,* but also their desire to keep alive at least some of the spirit and traditions of the *Old.* In the midst of change people remain even though, alas, time and "progress" has taken its toll. Of the old historic buildings of Turtle Bay, not one has survived the unending changes which have characterized the life of New York City. To what area of New York more than to Turtle Bay could better be applied the comments written in 1964 by Brooks Atkinson, "a journey-man who has come home."

By night, the splendor it flaunts is stunning. The sweep of lights in bright rows and in radiant parabolas that climb the sky is electrifying—emotionally as well as literally. All cities are superb at night because their hideous corners are devoured in darkness. But Manhattan can survive the daylight test. By day, it has the bizarre beauty of something that could not be imagined if the energy of a working community had not created it out of necessity.

* * *

The charm of Manhattan consists in the little congeries of aging houses, restaurants, candy stores, barber shops and bars, where individual communities maintain separate neighborhood lives. Although many of the neighborhoods exist amid some of the tallest buildings, it is difficult to perceive any relation between them. Boys play stickball in the streets, girls walk serenely home from church in dainty confirmation dresses, mothers trundle groceries home in carts from the corner store, and men tinker with their cars in the street as if the tallest building in the world were not soaring above them.

* * *

If Manhattan continues to be a place where people can live abundantly, the old neighborhoods are essential. A passing word to a neighbor on the street is more gratifying than a self-service elevator. But dehumanization may be the wave of the future. Some of the advance ripples have already come ashore. The elegant Grand Central Terminal, one of the treasures of the city, has been buried under a monstrous heap of office-space banality; and the noble Pennsylvania Station is being annihilated to make room for a sports arena. The vandals have a firm grip on Manhattan, with the acquiescence of the municipal Government and the community.
"But in the third century since the British took Nieuw Amsterdam from the Dutch and renamed it New York, the worldly borough of Manhattan is still a sovereign place that radiates energy and sharpens the minds of her people. Everything about Manhattan is alive."[17]

Carol singing in Amster Yard.

FOOTNOTES.

[1] Andrew Burnaby—English divine and traveller, born in 1732, published *Travels in North America, Journal of a Tour to Corsica,* etc. Died in 1812.

[2] Reprinted with permission of the *New York World-Telegram and Sun.*

[3] Margaret Fuller (1810–1850)—American writer and critic, friend of New England transcendentalists and associate of Horace Greeley on the *Tribune.*

[4] *Horace Greeley: Voice of the People* by William Harlan Hale. Harper & Brothers, N.Y., 1950.

[5] William Channing—(1810–1884)—Prominent Unitarian minister and author.

[6] *Israfel: The Life and Times of Edgar Allen Poe* by Hervey Allen. Holt, Rinehart and Winston, Inc., 1934.

[7] *Edgar Allen Poe* by Mary E. Phillips. Holt, Rinehart and Winston, Inc., 1926.

[8] Sholem Asch—Prominent Yiddish novelist, born in Poland and died a U.S. citizen. Among his novels are *The Nazarene* (1939), *The Apostle* (1943), *Mary* (1949), *A Passage in the Night* (1953), *The Prophet* (1955).

[9] Copyright 1946. *East River* by Sholem Asch, Putnam and Coward-McCann.

[10] Copyright 1929 by The New York Times Company. Reprinted with permission.

[11] Copyright 1949. From *Here Is New York* by E. B. White, Curtis Publishing Company. Reprinted with permission of the author and Harper & Row, Publishers.

[12] Copyright 1929 by The New York Times Company. Reprinted with permission.

[13] *The Letters of Thomas Wolfe,* Ed. Elizabeth Nowell, Scribner's, 1956.

[14] Copyright 1952 by The New York Times Company. Reprinted with permission.

[15] Copyright 1964 by The New York Times Company. Reprinted with permission.

[16] Copyright 1964 by The New York Times Company. Reprinted with permission.

[17] Copyright 1964 by The New York Times Company. Reprinted with permission.

BIBLIOGRAPHY.

Abbott, Berenice, and McCausland, Elizabeth, *Changing New York*. E. P. Dutton & Co., Inc., 1939.

Belden, E. Porter, *New York: Past, Present and Future.* G. P. Putnam, 1849.

Bonner, William T., *New York: The World's Metropolis, 1624–1924* . . . R. L. Polk & Co., 1924. (Bibliography.)

Booth, Mary L., *History of the City of New York From Its Earliest Settlement* . . . (2 vols.). Clark & Meeker, 1867.

Brendan Behan's New York, Bernard Geis Associates, 1964.

Brown, Henry Collins, *Valentine's Manual of the City of New York* (New Series). Valentine's Manual, Inc., 1916–1927.

In the Golden Nineties. Valentine's Manual, Inc., 1928.

Dayton, Abraham C., *Last Days of Knickerbocker Life in New York*, G. P. Putnam, 1897.

Despard, Matilda Pratt, *Old New York from the Battery to Bloomingdale.* G. P. Putnam's Sons, 1875.

Detmold, Mabel, *The Brownstones of Turtle Bay Gardens*, The East 49th Street Association, 1964.

Dilliard, Maud Esther, *An Album of New Netherland.* Twayne Publishers, Inc., 1963. (Bibliography.)

Dunlap, William, *History of the New Netherlands* . . . 1609–1789 (2 vols.). Carter & Thorp, 1839.

Dunshee, Kenneth Holcomb, *As You Pass By.* Hastings House, 1952.

Earle, Alice Morse, *Colonial Days in Old New York.* Charles Scribner's Sons, 1896.

Feininger and Lyman, *The Face of New York*, Crown Publishers, Inc., 1954.

Feininger and Simon, *New York*, The Viking Press, 1964.

Kelley, Frank Bergen, compiler, *Historical Guide to the City of New York.* Frederick A. Stokes Co., 1909. (Bibliographies.)

King, Moses, editor. *King's Handbook of New York City.* Moses King, 1892 (1893).

King's Views of New York—1908–1909. Moses King, 1908.

King's Photographic Views of New York . . . Moses King, 1895.

Kouwenhoven, John A., *The Columbia Historical Portrait of New York.* Doubleday & Company, Inc., 1953.

Lamb, Martha J., *History of the City of New York* . . . (2 vols.). A. S. Barnes & Co., 1877.

Laredo and Seitlin, *New York, People and Places*, Reinhold Publishing Corporation, 1964.

Leonard, John W., *History of the City of New York 1609–1909* (2 vols.). New York Journal of Commerce and Commercial Bulletin, 1910

Lewis, Emory, *Cue's New York*, Duell, Sloan & Pearce, 1963.

Little Old New York Illustrated. Oxford Publishing Company, 1910.

Look, editors of, in collaboration with Frederick Lewis Allen, *Look at America: New York City* (regional volume). Houghton Mifflin Company, 1948.

Look, editors of, *New York City*, Houghton Mifflin Company, 1956.

Lossing, Benson J., *History of New York City*, 1609–1884 (2 vols.). Perine Engraving & Publishing Co., 1884.

Lyman, Susan Elizabeth, *The Story of New York*, Crown Publishers, 1964.

Mayer, Grace, *Once Upon A City.* The Macmillan Company, 1958.

Moss, Frank, *The American Metropolis* . . . (3 vols.). Peter Fenelon Collier Press, 1897.

New York City Guide: A Comprehensive Guide to the Five Boroughs of the Metropolis . . . (American Guide Series, W.P.A.). Random House, 1939. (Historic houses indexed; bibliography.)

New York City Guide and Almanac, 1961–62. New York University Press, 1962. (Bibliography, pp. 109–112.)

New York Herald Tribune, editors of, *New York, New York*, The Dial Press, 1964.

Pritchett and Hofer, *New York Proclaimed*, Harcourt, Brace & World, Inc., 1965.

Stokes, Isaac Newton Phelps, *Iconography of Manhattan Island* (6 vols.). Robert H. Dodd, 1915–1928. (Bibliography.)

Valentine, David T., *History of the City of New York.* G. P. Putnam & Co., 1853. *Manual of the Common Council of New York* (26 vols.). *Valentine's Manuals*, various publishers, 1842–1867.

Van Pelt, Daniel, *Leslie's History of the Greater New York* (3 vols.). Arkell Publishing Co., 1898.

Van Rensselaer, Mrs. Schuyler, *History of the City of New York in the Seventeenth Century* (2 vols.). The Macmillan Company, 1909.

United Nations, *Your United Nations Official Guide Book*, New York, 1964.

PICTURE CREDITS.

Cover—courtesy of The New-York Historical Society

Frontispiece—courtesy of the United Nations

Opposite contents—courtesy of Kelly & Gruzen—Kahn and Jacobs, Associate Architects

Opposite page 1—from an engraving in *Valentine's Manual* published in 1861; courtesy of The New-York Historical Society

Page 2—engraved by W. W. Ryland; courtesy of The New-York Historical Society

Page 3—courtesy of the Beekman Family Association

Page 4—courtesy of The New-York Historical Society

Page 5—#1 water color by A. Hosier; courtesy of The New-York Historical Society
#2 from *Valentine's Manual* for 1857. Courtesy of The New-York Historical Society

Page 6—#1 engraved by A. H. Ritchie. Courtesy of The New-York Historical Society
#2 courtesy of The New-York Historical Society

Page 8—pen and ink drawing owned by Yale University; courtesy of Yale University and The New-York Historical Society

Page 9—engraving from *The American Revolution,* Vol. I, by John Fiske; courtesy of The New-York Historical Society

Page 10—courtesy of The New York Public Library

Page 12—oil on canvas by Samuel S. Osgood; courtesy of The New-York Historical Society

Page 13—#1 courtesy of The Museum of the City of New York
#2 from *Valentine's Manual,* 1858

Page 14—courtesy of The New-York Historical Society

Page 15—courtesy of The New-York Historical Society

Page 16—oil by A. Maris. Courtesy of The New-York Historical Society

Page 18—#1 from *Valentine's Manual,* 1861; courtesy of The New-York Historical Society
#2 from a contemporary drawing; courtesy of The New York Public Library

Page 19—Beekman portrait by Thomas LeClear; courtesy of The New-York Historical Society
#3 courtesy of The New York Public Library

Page 20—from *Frank Leslie's Illustrated Newspaper,* page 204, November 18, 1882; courtesy of The New-York Historical Society

Page 22—all courtesy of The New-York Historical Society

Page 25—courtesy of The Byron Collection, Museum of the City of New York

Page 26—#1 and #2 courtesy of Culver Pictures, Inc.
#3 courtesy of the Museum of the City of New York

Page 28—courtesy of Transcolor Corp., N.Y.

Page 30—#1 design by Michael Greer; photograph by Ernest M. Silva

Page 31—#2 and #3 courtesy of Mrs. Walter D. Binger; photograph by Peter N. Pruyn

Page 32—Copyright 1949, from *The Art of Living* by Saul Steinberg, Harper & Brothers, reproduced with the permission of Mr. Steinberg

Page 34—photograph by Nicholson Delaney

Page 35—photograph by Custom Studios

Page 36—courtesy of William Lescaze; photograph by Molitor

Page 37—designed by Michael Greer; photograph by Ernest M. Silva

Page 38—#1 courtesy of Culver Pictures, Inc.
#2 courtesy of United Press International, Inc.

Page 39—courtesy of United Press International, Inc. and Acme

Page 41—#1 Harold Sterner, architect; photograph by P. A. Dearborn
#2 photograph by Louis Reens

Page 43—courtesy of Polly Jackson and *The New York Herald Tribune Magazine*

Page 44—courtesy of the United Nations

Page 45—by British sculptress, Barbara Hepworth; courtesy of the United Nations

Page 46—courtesy of the United Nations

Page 47—courtesy of Culver Pictures, Inc.

Page 48—courtesy of United Press International, Inc. and Acme

Page 49—courtesy of Culver Pictures, Inc.

Page 50—by Danish sculptor, Heinrik Starcke; courtesy of the United Nations

Page 51—by French artist, Marc Chagall; courtesy of the United Nations

Page 52—courtesy of the United Nations

Page 53—courtesy of the United Nations

Page 54—#1 courtesy of the United Nations

Page 55—#2 by Yugoslav sculptor, Antun Augustincic; courtesy of the United Nations
#3 courtesy of the United Nations

Page 56—by Joseph N. Lacy, John Dinkeloo and Kevin Roche, principals of Eero Saarinen Associates; courtesy of the Ford Foundation; photograph by Ezra Stoller Associates

Page 57—Scheve, Lamb & Harmon Associates, architects, 1961

Page 58—courtesy of Alcoa Plaza Associates; photograph by Wagner International Photos

Page 59—courtesy Alcoa Plaza Associates

Page 60—George G. Sole, architect; photograph by Ernest Sisto; copyright 1965 by The New York Times Company. Reprinted with permission

Page 61—William Lescaze, architect; stained glass by Henry L. Willet; courtesy of William Lescaze and the National Council of Churches

Page 62—#1 Adams and Woodridge, architects; courtesy of the Episcopal Church Center

Page 63—#2 windows by Gabriel Loire; courtesy of the Episcopal Church Center; photograph by Peter N. Pruyn

Page 64—architects for Continental Can Building—Harrison and Abramowitz; courtesy of The Durst Organization; photograph by Lew Rosen

Page 66—courtesy of The New-York Historical Society

Page 67—John Mead Howells and Raymond Hood, architects; photograph courtesy of *The New York Daily News*

Page 68—William Lescaze, architect; photograph courtesy of William Lescaze

Page 69—sculpture by David Hare; photograph courtesy of David Hare

Page 70—#1 architects for Lorillard Building, Emery Roth & Sons; for Socony Mobil Building, Harrison and Abramowitz; photograph courtesy of The Durst Organization

Page 71—#2 architects, Emery Roth & Sons; photograph courtesy of The Durst Organization

Page 72—#1 courtesy of The Durst Organization; photograph by A. Devaney, Inc.

Page 73—#2 architects, Emery Roth & Sons; courtesy of The Durst Organization; photograph by Lew Rosen

Page 74—#1 courtesy of United States Plywood Company; photograph by Peter N. Pruyn

Page 75—#2 architectural sculpture by Beverly Pepper; courtesy of *The New York Herald Tribune Magazine*

Page 76—courtesy of the Museum of the City of New York

Page 79—photograph by Nicholson Delaney

Page 81—courtesy of James Amster; photograph by Owen Studios